Hello, I'm Your Bible

A Practical Guide to Accurately
Handling the Word of Truth

Jason Hardin

DeWard
Publishing Company

For Chloe

*I remember the look on your face the night you noticed
the North Star for the first time. May God's word always
serve as the North Star of your life.*

contents

acknowledgments

This book would not exist without the work of several who have significantly impacted my thinking.

Chapter 2 is adapted from a sermon delivered by Dee Bowman in Plainfield, Indiana. I still have my handwritten notes from that evening when I was seventeen years old.

Chapter 6 is based on a sermon outline by Edwin Crozier entitled, "Using the Standard Properly: Understanding Bible Genres." Much of Edwin's excellent work as a minister of the gospel is freely available at EdwinCrozier.com.

Several aspects of this material are an echo of Ferrell Jenkins' *Biblical Authority: Practical Lessons to Guide the Bible Student in Determining, Understanding and Applying Biblical Authority*. Published in 1990, that little book has since gone out-of-print. I'm particularly indebted to Jenkins for the charts that appear in Chapters 8 and 9 of this work.

Chapter 10 is adapted from an outstanding article by Jeff Smelser ("When Are Examples Binding?") that appeared in the February 2006 edition of *Biblical Insights*.

Since 1997, I have been adding snippets of helpful material to an ever-expanding file folder labeled, "The Bible: Its Nature and Importance." Undoubtedly, I have overlooked someone whose thoughts helped to shape some aspect of this work. I apologize in advance for any unintended oversights.

I am thankful for the many preachers and teachers who have molded within me a deep-seated respect for the sacred Scriptures. I will be particularly indebted to Steve Hardin (my father) and Aude McKee for the rest of my life. The sermons of these men were the first seeds of what you hold in your hands.

The meticulous proofreading and brotherly suggestions of

Nathan Williams were immeasurably helpful in producing this final product.

Finally, all glory and honor belongs to God. My prayer to him is that of the psalmist in Psalm 119.49. "Remember your word to your servant, in which you have made me hope."

preface

Could I ask you to do something before you turn the next page? I realize it's probably bad form to ask you to stop reading before you've even reached the first chapter, but this is important. I promise. Are you ready?

If at all possible, take a moment to pick up a Bible and be amazed. Amazed at what? At the fact that you are holding in your hands the very word of God. That is a breathtaking proposition, and its importance cannot be overstated. The Almighty Creator of the universe has told us what he wants us to know and preserved that communication in the form of a book.

We often do not appreciate what we have until it's gone. Where would we be without the Bible? How would we answer those foundational questions of origin, purpose and destiny? "Faith comes from hearing, and hearing through the word of Christ" (Rom 10.17). But what if there were nothing to hear? "Take the helmet of salvation, and the sword of the Spirit, which is the word of God" (Eph 6.17). But what if there were no sword?

How thankful we should be that "the sacred writings, which are able to make [us] wise for salvation through faith in Christ Jesus" are so freely available in our own language (2 Tim 3.15). How anxious we should be to apply our Lord's words in Matthew 4.4: "Man shall not live by bread alone, but by every word that comes from the mouth of God." In the language of Psalm 19.10, "More to be desired are [the words of God] than gold, even much fine gold."

The next time you pick up a Bible, don't forget to be amazed.

one

The World's Most Precious Book

In Psalm 16.11, David wrote of God, "You make known to me the path of life; in your presence there is fullness of joy; at your right hand are pleasures forevermore." There is a God. He is alive. In him we live and survive. From dust our God created man. He is our God, the great I AM. In Ephesians 1.3–6, the apostle Paul wrote,

> Blessed be the God and Father of our Lord Jesus Christ, who has blessed us in Christ with every spiritual blessing in the heavenly places, even as he chose us in him before the foundation of the world, that we should be holy and blameless before him. In love he predestined us for adoption as sons through Jesus Christ, according to the purpose of his will, to the praise of his glorious grace, with which he has blessed us in the Beloved.

This Creator-God had a plan before he ever laid the foundation of the world. His plan involved us—human beings whom he created in his image (Gen 1.27). His will for us is that we would be holy and blameless, as he is holy and blameless (1 Pet 1.14–16). In love he determined to make a way available, despite our rebellion against him, whereby we could be adopted as sons and daughters into his family through the sacrifice of his own Son, Jesus the Christ.

> You were dead in the trespasses and sins in which you once walked, following the course of this world, following the prince

of the power of the air, the spirit that is now at work in the sons of disobedience—among whom we all once lived in the passions of our flesh, carrying out the desires of the body and the mind, and were by nature children of wrath, like the rest of mankind. But God, being rich in mercy, because of the great love with which he loved us, even when we were dead in our trespasses, made us alive together with Christ—by grace you have been saved—and raised us up with him and seated us with him in the heavenly places in Christ Jesus, so that in the coming ages he might show the immeasurable riches of his grace in kindness toward us in Christ Jesus. For by grace you have been saved through faith. And this is not your own doing; it is the gift of God, not a result of works, so that no one may boast. For we are his workmanship, created in Christ Jesus for good works, which God prepared beforehand, that we should walk in them. (Eph 2.1–10)

I exist for the praise of God's glorious grace. You exist for the praise of God's glorious grace. He desires a relationship with each of us. He makes known to us the path of life. In his presence there is fullness of joy. At his right hand are pleasures forevermore.

God's Revelation of Himself to Mankind

God has powerfully revealed his magnificence to mankind via the creation of all things. Rebellious human beings ought to fearfully take note at each rising and setting of the sun.

For the wrath of God is revealed from heaven against all ungodliness and unrighteousness of men, who by their unrighteousness suppress the truth. For what can be known about God is plain to them, because God has shown it to them. For his invisible attributes, namely, his eternal power and divine nature, have been clearly perceived, ever since the creation of the world, in the things that have been made. So they are without excuse. (Rom 1.18–20)

As David poetically put it in Psalm 19.1–2,

The heavens declare the glory of God,
and the sky above proclaims his handiwork.

Day to day pours out speech,
> and night to night reveals knowledge.

And yet, the physical creation around us can only tell us so much. There is a God who has created all things, but who is he? What's he like? What about his character? Does he have any expectations of us? And how can we know if or when we've met them? Are there consequences for disobedience? Rewards for compliance? Is there a story and meaning behind our origin? Why are we here? What's life on this earth all about? What happens after we die?

The apostle Paul preached to the inhabitants of first-century Athens,

> "The God who made the world and everything in it, being Lord of heaven and earth, does not live in temples made by man, nor is he served by human hands, as though he needed anything, since he himself gives to all mankind life and breath and everything. And he made from one man every nation of mankind to live on all the face of the earth, having determined allotted periods and the boundaries of their dwelling place, that they should seek God, in the hope that they might feel their way toward him and find him. Yet he is actually not far from each one of us, for
>
> > 'In him we live and move and have our being';
> > as even some of your own poets have said,
> > 'For we are indeed his offspring.'" (Acts 17.24–28)

Paul did a great deal of preaching, from Jerusalem to Rome. But he is remembered most of all for what he wrote—thirteen books of what we refer to as the New Testament of the Bible. There is a God. He is alive. "By the word of the LORD the heavens were made, and by the breath of his mouth all their host" (Psa 33.6), but he has also provided a written revelation for all mankind—the means by which we can come to know him, follow him, and eventually live with him after death. "Your word," the psalmist wrote, "is a lamp to my feet and a light to my path" (Psa 119.105). The BIBLE could accurately be described as **B**asic **I**nstructions **B**efore **L**eaving **E**arth.

Notice just a few of the ways the words of God are described throughout the Bible.

But as for you, continue in what you have learned and have firmly believed, knowing from whom you learned it and how from childhood you have been acquainted with the **sacred writings**, which are able to make you wise for salvation through faith in Christ Jesus. All **Scripture** is **breathed out by God** and profitable for teaching, for reproof, for correction, and for training in righteousness, that the man of God may be competent, equipped for every good work. (2 Tim 3.14–17)

Sanctify them in the truth; **your word is truth.** (John 17.17)

Paul, a servant of Christ Jesus, called to be an apostle, set apart for the gospel of God, which he promised beforehand through his prophets in the **holy Scriptures...** (Rom 1.1–2)

For the **word of God** is **living** and **active, sharper than any two-edged sword**, piercing to the division of soul and of spirit, of joints and of marrow, and discerning the thoughts and intentions of the heart. And no creature is hidden from his sight, but all are naked and exposed to the eyes of him to whom we must give account. (Heb 4.12–13)

Do all things without grumbling or questioning, that you may be blameless and innocent, children of God without blemish in the midst of a crooked and twisted generation, among whom you shine as lights in the world, holding fast to **the word of life**, so that in the day of Christ I may be proud that I did not run in vain or labor in vain. (Phil 2.14–16)

Man shall not live by bread alone, but by **every word that comes from the mouth of God.** (Matt 4.4)

In all circumstances take up the shield of faith, with which you can extinguish all the flaming darts of the evil one; and take the helmet of salvation, and **the sword of the Spirit, which is the word of God**. (Eph 6.16–17)

For whatever was written in former days was **written for our instruction**, that through endurance and through **the encouragement of the Scriptures** we might have hope. (Rom 15.4)

> I write to you, fathers, because you know him who is from the beginning. I write to you, young men, because you are strong, and **the word of God** abides in you, and you have overcome the evil one. (1 John 2.14)

> Let **the word of Christ** dwell in you richly, teaching and admonishing one another in all wisdom, singing psalms and hymns and spiritual songs, with thankfulness in your hearts to God. (Col 3.16)

> Be diligent to present yourself approved to God as a workman who does not need to be ashamed, accurately handling **the word of truth**. (2 Tim 2.15, NASB)

> And we have something more sure, the **prophetic word**, to which you will do well to pay attention as to a lamp shining in a dark place, until the day dawns and the morning star rises in your hearts, knowing this first of all, that no prophecy of Scripture comes from someone's own interpretation. For no prophecy was ever produced by the will of man, but **men spoke from God** as they were **carried along by the Holy Spirit**. (2 Pet 1.19–21)

The Bible is not simply a collection of human thoughts about God. The Bible represents the very words of God himself. Therefore, our reaction to and handling of this book ought to be like that of the men and women whom Paul referenced in 1 Thessalonians 2.13.

> And we also thank God constantly for this, that when you received the word of God, which you heard from us, you accepted it not as the word of men but as what it really is, the word of God, which is at work in you believers.

If we truly desire insight into the deepest issues of existence—the character of God, the nature of humanity, God's intentions for the world, and where we go from here—no other source in the universe tells us so much, so accurately, as the written word of God.

Many Diverse Pieces, One Unified Book

We often refer to the Bible as one big book, but it's actually a collection of sixty-six different books broken down into two major sections—the Old and New Testaments. The sixty-six books could generally be grouped into a few basic categories.

Old Testament	New Testament
Law Genesis, Exodus, Leviticus, Numbers, Deuteronomy	**Gospels** Matthew, Mark, Luke, John
History Joshua, Judges, Ruth, 1 & 2 Samuel, 1 & 2 Kings, 1 & 2 Chronicles, Ezra, Nehemiah, Esther	**History** Acts of the Apostles
Poetry Job, Psalms, Proverbs, Ecclesiastes, Song of Solomon	**Letters** Romans, 1 & 2 Corinthians, Galatians, Ephesians, Philippians, Colossians, 1 & 2 Thessalonians, 1 & 2 Timothy, Titus, Philemon, Hebrews, James, 1 & 2 Peter, 1–3 John, Jude
Prophecy Isaiah, Jeremiah, Lamentations, Ezekiel, Daniel, Hosea, Joel, Amos, Obadiah, Jonah, Micah, Nahum, Habakkuk, Zephaniah, Haggai, Zechariah, Malachi	**Prophecy** Revelation

These sixty-six books were written over a period of about 1,600 years—a span of roughly 40 generations—by 40 different authors, men from vastly differing walks of life. For example:

Moses was a prince of Egypt who became a wilderness shepherd.
Peter was a fisherman.
Amos was a herdsman.
Joshua was a military general.
Nehemiah was a cup bearer for the king of Persia.
Daniel was a type of prime minister in the courts of Babylon.
Luke was a physician.
Solomon was a king and a philosopher.
Matthew was a tax collector.
Paul was a rabbi-in-training and a tentmaker.

These men wrote from vastly different places:

Moses, in the wilderness.
Jeremiah, in a dungeon.
Daniel, on a hillside and in a palace.
Paul, from prison.
Luke, while traveling.
John, in exile on the isle of Patmos.
Others, amidst the rigors of military campaigns.

They experienced times of war and times of peace. Some wrote from the heights of joy; others wrote from the depths of sorrow and despair. Some lived in Asia, others in Africa, and still others in Europe. They employed three different languages—Hebrew, Aramaic and Greek. They covered hundreds of topics—from the creation of all things to the complexity of human relationships; from the meaning of life to what can be expected after death.

The diversity of the Bible is remarkable—40 different authors over 1,600 years wrote 66 different books, from three different continents, in three different languages. And yet, there is astounding harmony and continuity, from Genesis to Revelation. Rather than an arbitrary book of random rules and incidental history, the greatest story ever told seamlessly unfolds from cover to cover. Paradise is lost in Genesis but is offered once again in Revelation. Mankind is banished from the Tree of Life in Genesis, but is beckoned to the Tree of Life with God in Revelation.

Imagine taking just ten authors—from the same walk of life, of the same generation, living in the same place, writing in the same language—and asking all ten to write a progressive account that harmonized and complimented its varying parts without any contradictions. The result would be a tangled mess of conflicting ideas and disjointed details.

There is only one explanation for the unity and cohesion of the Bible—one mind with one master plan. "For no prophecy was ever produced by the will of man, but men spoke from God as they were carried along by the Holy Spirit" (2 Pet 1.21). And what is that master plan? What is the Bible all about? **Rescue.** From Genesis to Revelation, God's written revelation is all about God's plan to rescue men and women from the ultimate problem of sin.

Our responsibility, therefore, is straightforward:

> Look carefully then how you walk, not as unwise but as wise, making the best use of the time, because the days are evil. Therefore do not be foolish, but understand what the will of the Lord is. (Eph 5.15–17)

Our responsibility is to discern and apply the truth as defined by our Creator. Even when it's not convenient. Even when it contradicts our current manner of life. Even when we must admit that we're wrong. Even when we must make difficult changes. Our responsibility is to discern and apply the truth, because only the truth can set us free (John 8.32).

If you want to learn more about the Bible but have no clue where to start, this book is for you. If you know a great deal about the Bible but your relationship with the written word has grown stale, this book is for you. If you read the Bible regularly and are determined to grow in your ability to share the will of God with others, this book is for you.

Questions for Growth and Discussion

1. When Paul used the phrase "sacred writings" in 2 Timothy 3.15, what did he mean?

2. What is meant in 2 Timothy 3.16 by "all Scripture is breathed out by God"?

3. In Romans 1.1–2, when Paul referenced "the holy Scriptures," what did he mean?

4. How is the word of God "living and active, sharper than any two-edged sword, piercing to the division of soul and of spirit, of joints and of marrow, and discerning the thoughts and intentions of the heart" (Heb 4.12)?

5. Why would Paul describe God's written revelation as "the word of life" in Philippians 2.16?

6. In what way is the word of God "the sword of the Spirit" (Eph 6.17)?

7. In your own words, what is the message of Romans 15.4?

8. Practically speaking, how does "the word of Christ" come to "dwell in us" (Col 3.16)?

9. Why is it vital that we learn how to "accurately handle" the word of truth (2 Tim 2.15)?

10. What is the message of 2 Peter 1.21? What are the implications if it is true?

two

If It's Breathed-Out by God...

Few passages serve as a better gateway from the words on the printed pages of our Bibles into the realm of practical application than Paul's encouragement in 2 Timothy 3.14–17:

> But as for you, continue in what you have learned and have firmly believed, knowing from whom you learned it and how from childhood you have been acquainted with the sacred writings, which are able to make you wise for salvation through faith in Christ Jesus. All Scripture is breathed out by God and profitable for teaching, for reproof, for correction, and for training in righteousness, that the man of God may be competent, equipped for every good work.

This is a significant passage of Scripture for a number of reasons. It's absolutely packed with implications and ramifications.

"All Scripture Is Inspired by God"

That's how most of our English translations of the Bible render Paul's words to Timothy. The English Standard Version quite accurately captures Paul's vivid language as it reads in the original Greek—"All Scripture is breathed out by God." The implication? Paul's material came not from the mind of Paul but from the mind of God.

In our English language, we have certain words or parts of words that are referred to as *sibilant* sounds—sounds that are formed by storing up a little bit of air and then hissing out that air over our tongues, past our teeth and lips. We hear them as soft "C" and "S" sounds.

For example, say the word *suit* out loud. Don't just read it. Say it!

The same thing with *sibilant* ... and *sound* ... and *same*. Those are sibilant sounds.

Now, try to say the word *suit* without exhaling. Go ahead, try it!

You can't do it, can you? In order to say the word *suit*, you have to exhale.

We also have what are referred to as *plosive* sounds in English. This word is remarkably close to the word *explosion*, and there's a reason. A plosive sound is a type of mini-explosion off our lips that forms "P" sounds, "B" sounds, and "D" sounds.

Say *Peter* out loud and, as you do, put your hand directly in front of your mouth.

There was a little explosion of air off your lips, wasn't there? Now try to say *Peter* without exhaling ... ... you can't do it, can you? And there's a simple reason. Spoken language is formed as we inhale and exhale. We can't engage in audible speech without breathing.

Now, think about that simple principle as it relates to 2 Timothy 3 of the Bible. Paul wants to make this point abundantly clear. What Timothy received, what Paul wrote to individual Christians and churches all over the world, what has been preserved for thousands of years, what we're getting to know in this book—was God-breathed. It wasn't dreamed up by Paul. It didn't originate in the mind of any man but in the mind of God.

That fact coincides perfectly with what Jesus said to his apostles just prior to his death.

> These things I have spoken to you while I am still with you. But the Helper, the Holy Spirit, whom the Father will send in my name, he will teach you all things and bring to your remembrance all that I have said to you. (John 14.25–26)

> But when the Helper comes, whom I will send to you from the Father, the Spirit of truth, who proceeds from the Father, he will bear witness about me. (John 15.26)

I still have many things to say to you, but you cannot bear them now. When the Spirit of truth comes, he will guide you into all the truth, for he will not speak on his own authority, but whatever he hears he will speak, and he will declare to you the things that are to come. (John 16.12–13)

This is the very idea of **inspiration**—God will put the sibilant and plosive communication, the verbiage, the nouns and pronouns, the thoughts and expressions into the minds of chosen men.

In 1 Corinthians 2.1–5 Paul wrote,

And I, when I came to you, brothers, did not come proclaiming to you the testimony of God with lofty speech or wisdom. For I decided to know nothing among you except Jesus Christ and him crucified. And I was with you in weakness and in fear and much trembling, and my speech and my message were not in plausible words of wisdom, but in demonstration of the Spirit and of power, that your faith might not rest in the wisdom of men but in the power of God.

And so, Paul was able to make the claim that he did in Romans 10.17—"Faith comes from hearing, and hearing through the word of Christ." Not the words of Paul but the words of Christ! God communicated what he wanted communicated and inspired men recorded it for all time.

As it is written,

"What no eye has seen, nor ear heard,
    nor the heart of man imagined,
what God has prepared for those who love him"—

these things God has revealed to us through the Spirit. For the Spirit searches everything, even the depths of God. (1 Cor 2.9–10)

Mankind could not possibly concoct the means of his own salvation. Regardless of all our human inventiveness, skill, and wisdom, we cannot find or articulate the means of our own salvation from sin. There is no river we can ford, no mountain we can climb; on our own, we're doomed. We need something more.

> Among the mature we do impart wisdom, although it is not a wisdom of this age or of the rulers of this age, who are doomed to pass away. But we impart a secret and hidden wisdom of God, which God decreed before the ages for our glory. (1 Cor 2.6–7)

And the ultimate result is that we have an inspired (God-breathed) collection of communications from the Creator of the universe to mankind. "We have the mind of Christ" (1 Cor 2.16).

> For we did not follow cleverly devised myths when we made known to you the power and coming of our Lord Jesus Christ, but we were eyewitnesses of his majesty. For when he received honor and glory from God the Father, and the voice was borne to him by the Majestic Glory, "This is my beloved Son, with whom I am well pleased," we ourselves heard this very voice borne from heaven, for we were with him on the holy mountain. And we have something more sure, the prophetic word, to which you will do well to pay attention as to a lamp shining in a dark place, until the day dawns and the morning star rises in your hearts, knowing this first of all, that no prophecy of Scripture comes from someone's own interpretation. For no prophecy was ever produced by the will of man, but men spoke from God as they were carried along by the Holy Spirit. (2 Pet 1.16–21)

Which leads us finally to Paul's words in Ephesians 3.1–5.

> For this reason I, Paul, a prisoner for Christ Jesus on behalf of you Gentiles—assuming that you have heard of the stewardship of God's grace that was given to me for you, how the mystery was made known to me by revelation, as I have written briefly. When you read this, you can perceive my insight into the mystery of Christ, which was not made known to the sons of men in other generations as it has now been revealed to his holy apostles and prophets by the Spirit.

"What I got," Paul claimed, "I got from the Holy Spirit of God. He prodded me, carried me along, and told me what to write... so I wrote it down. Now, when you read it, you can know exactly what I know about God's will for your life." All Scripture is breathed out by God.

"All Scripture is Profitable"

The word *profitable* is defined as "yielding profit; beneficial or useful." Imagine that, as you're driving down Main Street this week, you see a sign outside of a bank advertising **"10% Profit Guaranteed."** You stop the car, walk into the bank, and tell the nice lady behind the teller's counter, "I came for my profit." She asks for your name, you tell her, and she begins to look confused as she scans her computer screen. She asks if you go by a different name, and you say "No." She finally says, "I'm sorry, but I'm not seeing any bank account attached to that name." With a smile you tell her, "I don't have a bank account here. I just saw the sign—10% Profit Guaranteed—that sounded good to me, so I decided to come inside, and now I'd like my profit."

We know how that nice teller would respond. "You mean to tell me that you came here looking for your profit, but you don't have anything in this bank?" The reason for her question is absolutely obvious—you're not going to get any kind of profit until you invest something!

And with that in mind, remember what the Spirit said in 2 Timothy 3. "All Scripture is breathed out by God and profitable." Profitable for whom? For those who **invest** in it. You can't get anything out of the word of God without some investigation. You can't get any profit from the word of God without investing your time and enthusiasm and effort into the things it says. You've got to find out what it says for yourself!

And if you do, you'll discover there is no treasure, nothing you can acquire or own, nothing that is comparable with investing in God's word. The Holy Spirit didn't make a mistake when he used that word. God's word is profitable. But in what way, practically speaking, is all of Scripture profitable?

"All Scripture is Profitable for Doctrine"

Doctrine simply means "teaching." Jesus made that point clear as he spoke of the Pharisees and scribes from Jerusalem in Matthew 15.7–9.

> You hypocrites! Well did Isaiah prophesy of you, when he said:
>
> "This people honors me with their lips,
>> but their heart is far from me;
> in vain do they worship me,
>> teaching as doctrines the commandments of men."

Doctrine is teaching. All Scripture is profitable for teaching. But teaching about what?

Have you ever looked up at the clouds in disappointment or despair or confusion and asked, "What is this all about, anyway?" "Who am I?" "Why me?" "Why am I here?" "What am I supposed to be doing?" There is good news. God's word is profitable! It answers those most fundamental questions. We can study medicine, philosophy, psychiatry, biology and all sorts of other human fields, but we won't find the answers to those bedrock questions of human existence. Not in any Encyclopedia or medical journal. Not in any book of human wisdom. Not online. With each of those sources, we're dealing with the limitations of human experience and wisdom.

But God has provided the answers to those questions that so often keep us awake at night. "Why am I here?" "Who am I?" "Where am I going?" He led Solomon to write in Ecclesiastes 12.13–14,

> The end of the matter; all has been heard. Fear God and keep his commandments, for this is the whole duty of man. For God will bring every deed into judgment, with every secret thing, whether good or evil.

Who am I? "Fear God."

Why am I here? "Keep his commandments."

Where am I going? "For God will bring every deed into judgment."

The Scriptures are God-breathed. They identify sin. They teach us what to do about sin. They give insight into the nature of human relationships. They empower us to maintain the kind of faith that is productive of the highest aspirations. They encourage us to persevere in the midst of a dark and dying culture. They guide us along the paths of abundant life. How dare we not consult the God-breathed Scriptures! The Bible is the Book of Life. It's the textbook for who we are. It's the recipe. The roadmap. It's everything we need.

"All Scripture is Profitable for Reproof"

To *reprove* means "to convict." The word of God convicts us of sin, but it also convicts us of the existence and preciousness of Jesus Christ. God's word masterfully cuts us to the core as sinful creatures. We're rebellious and unholy in the sight of our patient and holy Creator. But his word also reveals God's eternal plan to provide a Savior. Having been convicted of our need for such a Savior, we're naturally led to ask, "What shall we do?" (Acts 2.37)

Hebrews 11.1 reads, "Now faith is the assurance of things hoped for, the conviction of things not seen." The more I learn of God's revealed will, the more I become intimately acquainted with my own sinful demise. I've wallowed in the mud and muck of my own filth, and there is nothing I can do to rescue myself. Scripture is perfectly designed by God to provide the reproof needed to jolt me to a desperate awareness of my fatal spiritual condition. The only question is, will I invest in the reproof it provides?

"All Scripture is Profitable for Correction"

Correction literally means "to make straight again." God's word gives us a means of correction. It reveals the gospel plan of salvation—God's rescue operation on behalf of his image-bearers. And Scripture is designed by God to be a life-long corrective measure. Living for God as a disciple of Jesus Christ is like keeping your vehicle between the ditches, inside the lines of the highway. Living for God involves making continual, never-ending, little corrective measures that are intended to keep the vehicles of our lives going straight.

If you ever spent any significant time on a large body of water before the days of computers, you probably saw the instruments involved in getting from Point-A to Point-B. Men who wanted to safely travel long distances across the water would use maps and instruments that enabled them to draw (and travel by) straight lines. As they drew the line of their trajectory and compared their present direction with their desired destination, they were able to quickly and efficiently discover what adjustments they needed to make in their heading.

Everyone knows that the shortest course from here to there is a straight line. You might discover that you're presently just ⅛ of a mile off-course. You might have a friend who reasons, "Don't worry about it. We can see for miles." But the wise pilot shakes his head and takes the time to correct his course. If you're ⅛ of a mile off now and you continue on that straight line, by the time you get where you had hoped to be going, you'll find that you are many miles away from the port.

God's word is our beacon. Our "True North." Our frame of reference. If we lock on to it, we'll end up where we want to go. But if we turn away from it and pave our own trail, we're guaranteed to get off-course. It may seem like the slimmest of margins in the moment, but it can eventually cost us everything!

"All Scripture is Profitable for Training in Righteousness"

God's word not only tells me how to correct my course but how to stay on course. It trains me in "right-way-ness."

> Your word is a lamp to my feet
> and a light to my path.
> I have sworn an oath and confirmed it,
> to keep your righteous rules.
> I am severely afflicted;
> give me life, O Lord, according to your word!

Accept my freewill offerings of praise, O Lord,
    and teach me your rules.
I hold my life in my hand continually,
    but I do not forget your law.
The wicked have laid a snare for me,
    but I do not stray from your precepts.
Your testimonies are my heritage forever,
    for they are the joy of my heart.
I incline my heart to perform your statutes
    forever, to the end. (Psa 119.105–112)

God created his word with the power to train men and women to walk in the ways that are right, as defined by their Creator. But the principle behind training is the same principle we noted behind investments. In order to get something out of training, you have to put something into it. I can't train for you, and you can't train for me. If there is profit that comes from training, it comes only with diligent, hard, personal work.

How "Complete" Are You?

"All Scripture is breathed out by God and profitable for teaching, for reproof, for correction, and for training in righteousness, that the man of God may be competent, equipped for every good work" (2 Tim 3.16–17). It's time for some honest inventory. What's missing in your life? Do you feel complete? Competent? Fully equipped as you face each new day? If not, could the reason be that you aren't taking full advantage of the revealed will of God for your life?

Questions for Growth and Discussion

1. Reread Jesus' promises in John 14.25–26, 15.26 and 16.12–13. In your own words, what is he promising his apostles?

2. Why is it so important that our faith not rest in the wisdom of men but in the power of God (1 Cor 2.1–5)? Practically speaking, how does that happen?

3. Why did Paul refer to what he was imparting as "secret and hidden wisdom" (1 Cor 2.6–7)?

4. In your own words, what is Paul saying in Ephesians 3.4?

5. In everyday real life, how can we "invest" in the word of God so that we can expect it to be "profitable" for our time on the earth?

6. Doctrine is teaching. Take a few moments to list some of the significant doctrines from God's word that have shaped your life. Are there specific Scriptures you can list to show why you believe those doctrines?

7. How have you been reproved by the Scriptures in the past?

8. Correction literally means "to make straight again." Is there anything in your life that needs to be "made straight again"?

9. Can you rephrase the basic message of Psalm 119.105–112?

10. If I am to be trained by God-breathed Scripture, what sort of attitude do I need to have?

three

Distinguishing Between the Covenants

Having established that God's written revelation to mankind is precious and profitable, we move into the realm of application. Remember, the master plan behind the Bible is rescue. From Genesis to Revelation, God's book is all about God's plan to rescue men and women from the ultimate problem of sin. Our responsibility begins with discernment.

> Look carefully then how you walk, not as unwise but as wise, making the best use of the time, because the days are evil. Therefore do not be foolish, but **understand** what the will of the Lord is. (Eph 5.15–17)

Notice what we can logically deduce just from Ephesians 5.17. There is a Lord over humanity. This Lord has a will. His will can be understood. To live in willful ignorance of or rebellion against the will of the Lord is foolish.

The rest of this book is aimed at equipping us to live up to the Spirit's expectation expressed in Ephesians 5.15–17. God's written revelation to mankind is precious and profitable. Therefore, we would be wise to understand and apply it to our lives. And few things are more foundational to our understanding of God's will for our lives than to notice the Spirit-drawn contrast between the covenants of the Bible.

Covenants

A *covenant* can most easily be defined as "a relationship based on promises." Promises are often made between neighbors, friends, the rulers of different nations, and so on. The essence of a covenant is an understanding—this is what you can expect from me; this is what I expect from you. Such covenants between men existed throughout the Old Testament. In Genesis 31.44–45, Laban said to his nephew Jacob,

> Come now, let us make a **covenant**, you and I. And let it be a witness between you and me." So Jacob took a stone and set it up as a pillar.

In 1 Samuel 18.1–3, we read of Jonathan, the son of King Saul, and his close relationship with David:

> As soon as he had finished speaking to Saul, the soul of Jonathan was knit to the soul of David, and Jonathan loved him as his own soul. And Saul took him that day and would not let him return to his father's house. Then Jonathan made a **covenant** with David, because he loved him as his own soul.

Even the marriages between men and women are described by God in the context of a covenant.

> And this second thing you do. You cover the LORD's altar with tears, with weeping and groaning because he no longer regards the offering or accepts it with favor from your hand. But you say, "Why does he not?" Because the LORD was witness between you and the wife of your youth, to whom you have been faithless, though she is your companion and your wife by **covenant**. (Mal 2.13–14)

One of the special things about the Bible is that it records, defines, and encourages covenant relationships between human beings and God. In fact, the overarching themes of both the Old and New Testaments are set within the framework of two major covenants—the law delivered through Moses in the Old Testament, and the gospel of Jesus Christ in the New Testament. We'll talk more about those in a moment.

Covenant Relationships with God in the Old Testament

On different occasions throughout the Old Testament, the Creator pledged himself and his blessings by promises to people. One of the earliest references to a covenant in the Bible occurs in the story of Noah and the flood. In Genesis 6.17–18, God told Noah,

> For behold, I will bring a flood of waters upon the earth to destroy all flesh in which is the breath of life under heaven. Everything that is on the earth shall die. But I will establish my **covenant** with you, and you shall come into the ark, you, your sons, your wife, and your sons' wives with you.

Following the flood, in Genesis 9.8–17,

> Then God said to Noah and to his sons with him, "Behold, I establish my **covenant** with you and your offspring after you, and with every living creature that is with you, the birds, the livestock, and every beast of the earth with you, as many as came out of the ark; it is for every beast of the earth. I establish my **covenant** with you, that never again shall all flesh be cut off by the waters of the flood, and never again shall there be a flood to destroy the earth." And God said, "This is the sign of the **covenant** that I make between me and you and every living creature that is with you, for all future generations: I have set my bow in the cloud, and it shall be a sign of the **covenant** between me and the earth. When I bring clouds over the earth and the bow is seen in the clouds, I will remember my **covenant** that is between me and you and every living creature of all flesh. And the waters shall never again become a flood to destroy all flesh. When the bow is in the clouds, I will see it and remember the everlasting **covenant** between God and every living creature of all flesh that is on the earth." God said to Noah, "This is the sign of the **covenant** that I have established between me and all flesh that is on the earth."

God defined his relationship with mankind based on a promise—never again to destroy the world and all of its inhabitants by water. He placed the rainbow in the sky as a sign and reminder of his covenant with the earth and every living thing. But the covenant was accompanied by a code of conduct for Noah and his descendants.

> And God blessed Noah and his sons and said to them, "Be fruitful and multiply and fill the earth. The fear of you and the dread of you shall be upon every beast of the earth and upon every bird of the heavens, upon everything that creeps on the ground and all the fish of the sea. Into your hand they are delivered. Every moving thing that lives shall be food for you. And as I gave you the green plants, I give you everything. But you shall not eat flesh with its life, that is, its blood. And for your lifeblood I will require a reckoning: from every beast I will require it and from man. From his fellow man I will require a reckoning for the life of man.
>
> > Whoever sheds the blood of man,
> >   by man shall his blood be shed,
> > for God made man in his own image.
>
> And you, be fruitful and multiply, teem on the earth and multiply in it." (Gen 9.1–7)

God established a covenant with mankind after the flood—a relationship based on promises. In essence he said, "This is what you can expect from me; this is what I expect from you."

Years later, in Genesis 12.1–3, God made further promises to a man named Abram.

> Now the LORD said to Abram, "Go from your country and your kindred and your father's house to the land that I will show you. And I will make of you a great nation, and I will bless you and make your name great, so that you will be a blessing. I will bless those who bless you, and him who dishonors you I will curse, and in you all the families of the earth shall be blessed."

God desired a working relationship with Abram. He wanted to use Abram as a part of his ultimate rescue plan, and he intended to bless Abram in the process.

When Abram was ninety-nine years old the LORD appeared to Abram and said to him, "I am God Almighty; walk before me, and be blameless, that I may make my **covenant** between me and you, and may multiply you greatly." Then Abram fell on his face. And God said to him, "Behold, my **covenant** is with you, and you shall be the father of a multitude of nations. No longer shall your name be called Abram, but your name shall be Abraham, for I have made you the father of a multitude of nations. I will make you exceedingly fruitful, and I will make you into nations, and kings shall come from you. And I will establish my **covenant** between me and you and your offspring after you throughout their generations for an everlasting **covenant**, to be God to you and to your offspring after you. And I will give to you and to your offspring after you the land of your sojournings, all the land of Canaan, for an everlasting possession, and I will be their God."

And God said to Abraham, "As for you, you shall keep my **covenant**, you and your offspring after you throughout their generations. This is my **covenant**, which you shall keep, between me and you and your offspring after you: Every male among you shall be circumcised. You shall be circumcised in the flesh of your foreskins, and it shall be a sign of the **covenant** between me and you." (Gen 17.1–11)

Once again, God was willing to establish a special relationship with Abraham—a covenant based on promises. "This is what you can expect from me; this is what I expect from you."

The books of Genesis and Exodus chronicle the growth of the descendants of Abraham into a nation. Eventually, God raised up a leader in Moses and communicated with the people through him. God delivered this people from Egyptian bondage. He protected them and provided for them in the wilderness. He guided them to Mount Sinai and powerfully reminded them of their recent past—his deliverance of them, his fighting and providing for them. And on this basis of what they had seen and heard, he offered them a national covenant—a relationship based on promises.

Thus you shall say to the house of Jacob, and tell the people of Israel: You yourselves have seen what I did to the Egyptians, and how I bore you on eagles' wings and brought you to myself. Now therefore, if you will indeed obey my voice and keep my **covenant**, you shall be my treasured possession among all peoples, for all the earth is mine; and you shall be to me a kingdom of priests and a holy nation. These are the words that you shall speak to the people of Israel.

So Moses came and called the elders of the people and set before them all these words that the LORD had commanded him. All the people answered together and said, "All that the LORD has spoken we will do." And Moses reported the words of the people to the LORD. (Exod 19.3–8)

God offered a covenant to Abraham's descendants—a relationship based on promises. "This is what you can expect from me; this is what I expect from you." The people agreed, and God gave them a law.

But if you're familiar at all with the Old Testament, you know that a prevailing theme from Exodus forward is Israel's failure to live up to the terms of their covenant with God. He punished and disciplined them over and over again. They would cry out for mercy, and he would deliver them, only to watch as they returned to the filth of their unrighteousness. They deserved to be abandoned by God and obliterated for their rebellious negligence.

And yet, God had made a promise—a promise that went back all the way to the days of Abraham—and God is faithful. Because of the covenant he had made with Abraham, Abraham's seed would not be completely cast off, even when they failed to live by the covenant agreement. Through the darkest of times, God's grace continued to wait for and, finally, to exhort a faithful remnant to stand strong. Listen to his very personal, heartfelt words in Isaiah 55.1–3, 6–7.

Come, everyone who thirsts,
    come to the waters;
and he who has no money,
    come, buy and eat!

Come, buy wine and milk
    without money and without price.
Why do you spend your money for that which is not bread,
    and your labor for that which does not satisfy?
Listen diligently to me, and eat what is good,
    and delight yourselves in rich food.
Incline your ear, and come to me;
    hear, that your soul may live;
and I will make with you an everlasting covenant,
    my steadfast, sure love for David.

Seek the LORD while he may be found;
    call upon him while he is near;
let the wicked forsake his way,
    and the unrighteous man his thoughts;
let him return to the LORD, that he may have compassion
    on him,
    and to our God, for he will abundantly pardon.

New Testament Commentary on God's Covenant with Israel

The New Testament, in several places, establishes a fundamental change in God's dealing with humanity—a difference between God's covenant with Israel and a new covenant made available to all men and women through Jesus Christ.

Or do you not know, brothers—for I am speaking to those who know the law—that the law is binding on a person only as long as he lives? For a married woman is bound by law to her husband while he lives, but if her husband dies she is released from the law of marriage. Accordingly, she will be called an adulteress if she lives with another man while her husband is alive. But if her husband dies, she is free from that law, and if she marries another man she is not an adulteress.

Likewise, my brothers, **you also have died to the law through the body of Christ, so that you may belong to another, to him who has been raised from the dead,** in order that we may bear fruit for God. For while we were living in the flesh, our sinful passions, aroused by the law, were at work in our members to bear fruit for death. But now **we are released from the law, having died to that which held us captive, so that we serve in the new way of the Spirit and not in the old way of the written code.** (Rom 7.1–6)

Such is the confidence that we have through Christ toward God. Not that we are sufficient in ourselves to claim anything as coming from us, but our sufficiency is from God, who has made us competent to be ministers of **a new covenant**, not of the letter but of the Spirit. For the letter kills, but the Spirit gives life. (2 Cor 3.4–6)

Now before faith came, we were held captive under the law, imprisoned until the coming faith would be revealed. So then, the law was our guardian **until Christ came**, in order that we might be justified by faith. But now that faith has come, **we are no longer under a guardian**, for in Christ Jesus you are all sons of God, through faith. For as many of you as were baptized into Christ have put on Christ. There is neither Jew nor Greek, there is neither slave nor free, there is no male and female, for you are all one in Christ Jesus. And if you are Christ's, then you are Abraham's offspring, heirs according to promise. (Gal 3.26–29)

Therefore remember that at one time you Gentiles in the flesh, called "the uncircumcision" by what is called the circumcision, which is made in the flesh by hands—remember that you were at that time separated from Christ, alienated from the commonwealth of Israel and **strangers to the covenants of promise**, having no hope and without God in the world. But now in Christ Jesus you who once were far off have **been brought near** by the blood of Christ. For he himself is our peace, who has made us both one and has broken down in his flesh the dividing wall of hostility by abolishing the law of commandments expressed in ordinances, that he might create in himself **one new man** in place of the two, so making peace, and might reconcile us both to God in one body through the cross, thereby killing the hostility. (Eph 2.11–16)

In particular, the New Testament book of Hebrews extensively addresses the difference between the old and new covenants. If Hebrews has one key word, it's *better*. In the introductory section of the book, the writer shows that Jesus is a better messenger than either the prophets or the angels (Heb 1). As the apostle and high priest of our confession, he is better than Moses (Heb 3). He provides a better rest than was provided by Joshua (Heb 4). He is a better priest than were the Levites (Heb 5–7). Based on that better foundation, Hebrews 8 expounds on the better covenant made available through Jesus, which is established on better promises.

Why was a new covenant enacted? "For if that first covenant had been faultless, there would have been no occasion to look for a second" (Heb 8.7). The first covenant involved two parties: God, who was represented by the law, and the people of Israel. Neither God nor his law were at fault. "The law is holy, and the commandment is holy and righteous and good" (Rom 7.12). The fault was with the people who failed to keep the covenant instituted at Sinai.

For **he** finds fault with **them** when he says:

> "Behold, the days are coming, declares the Lord, when I will establish a new covenant with the house of Israel and with the house of Judah, not like the covenant that I made with their fathers on the day when I took them by the hand to bring them out of the land of Egypt. For they did not continue in my covenant, and so I showed no concern for them, declares the Lord." (Heb 8.8–9)

The New Testament clearly establishes that the Mosaic law had a purpose. But when that purpose was fulfilled, there was no longer a need for the old law.

> Why then the law? It was added because of transgressions, until the offspring should come to whom the promise had been made, and it was put in place through angels by an intermediary. Now an intermediary implies more than one, but God is one.
>
> Is the law then contrary to the promises of God? Certainly not! For if a law had been given that could give life, then righteousness would indeed be by the law. But the Scripture impris-

oned everything under sin, so that the promise by faith in Jesus Christ might be given to those who believe.

Now before faith came, we were held captive under the law, imprisoned until the coming faith would be revealed. So then, **the law was our guardian until Christ came**, in order that we might be justified by faith. But now that faith has come, **we are no longer under a guardian**, for in Christ Jesus you are all sons of God, through faith. (Gal 3.19–26)

The old law of Moses is no longer in effect. The covenant of God with Abraham's descendants has served its purpose. Christ has come, and we are no longer under that Old Testament guardian.

The New Covenant was a Fulfillment of Old Testament Prophecy

A key section of Scripture in the discussion of the change in covenants is God's words through his prophet Jeremiah who prophesied from 627–586 BC. In Jeremiah 31.31–34, God's inspired spokesman declared,

> Behold, the days are coming, declares the LORD, when I will make **a new covenant** with the house of Israel and the house of Judah, not like the covenant that I made with their fathers on the day when I took them by the hand to bring them out of the land of Egypt, my covenant that they broke, though I was their husband, declares the LORD. But this is the covenant that I will make with the house of Israel after those days, declares the LORD: I will put my law within them, and I will write it on their hearts. And I will be their God, and they shall be my people. And no longer shall each one teach his neighbor and each his brother, saying, 'Know the LORD,' for they shall all know me, from the least of them to the greatest, declares the LORD. For I will forgive their iniquity, and I will remember their sin no more.

Jeremiah's words from hundreds of years before are the basis of the quotation in Hebrews 8 of the New Testament.

Now the point in what we are saying is this: we have such a high priest, one who is seated at the right hand of the throne of the Majesty in heaven, a minister in the holy places, in the true tent that the Lord set up, not man... As it is, Christ has obtained a ministry that is as much more excellent than the old as the covenant he mediates is better, since it is enacted on better promises. (Heb 8.1–2, 6)

As is summarized in Hebrews 8.13, "In speaking of a new covenant, he makes the first one obsolete. And what is becoming obsolete and growing old is ready to vanish away." The old covenant with Israel that had been founded on the law delivered through Moses came to a close at Christ's crucifixion.

Therefore he is the mediator of a new covenant, so that those who are called may receive the promised eternal inheritance, since a death has occurred that redeems them from the transgressions committed under the first covenant. For where a will is involved, the death of the one who made it must be established. For a will takes effect only at death, since it is not in force as long as the one who made it is alive. (Heb 9.15–17)

The old record of debt, legal demands, and wall of separation between Jew and Gentile were "set aside," having been nailed to the cross (Col 2.13–15). As a civil institution, Judaism would soon be forever altered with the destruction of Jerusalem and its temple in AD 70. God's special covenant with Old Testament Israel had served its greatest eternal purpose in the life, death, burial, and resurrection of Jesus as the Lamb provided by God to take away the sin of the world (John 1.29).

Vital Features of the New Covenant

On this historical side of the cross, the writer of Hebrews assures us that the new covenant of Jesus Christ is "better, since it is enacted on better promises" (Heb 8.6). But in what ways is it "better"? The inspired New Testament writer roots his argument in the prophecy of Jeremiah 31 and specifically recalls three outstanding features to make his "better" case.

1. **Under the new covenant, there is renewed emphasis on the inner man.**

> For this is the covenant that I will make with the house of Israel after those days, declares the Lord: I will put my laws into their minds, and write them on their hearts, and I will be their God, and they shall be my people. (Heb 8.10)

The precepts of the new covenant go much deeper than words carved on tablets of stone. God's relationship based on promises with Christians is emblazoned on tablets of human hearts (2 Cor 3.3). Our very wills—not simply our outward actions—are to be subjected to and harmonized with the revealed will of God.

2. **Every subject of the new covenant knows the Lord.**

> And they shall not teach, each one his neighbor and each one his brother, saying, 'Know the Lord,' for they shall all know me, from the least of them to the greatest. (Heb 8.11)

Old Testament descendants of Abraham were born, circumcised on the eighth day as a sign of their covenant relationship with God, and later enlightened about the nature of the covenant of which they were already a part as they progressed in age (Deut 6.4–9). The men and women of the new covenant of Jesus Christ know the Lord. They hear, learn, and personally respond for themselves to God's gracious offer of covenant relationship (John 6.45). "From the least of them to the greatest," they are "a chosen race, a royal priesthood, a holy nation, a people for his own possession" (1 Pet 2.9).

3. **Under the new covenant, children of God can experience absolute and complete forgiveness.**

> For I will be merciful toward their iniquities, and I will remember their sins no more. (Heb 8.12)

Make careful note of this crucial point made in Hebrews 10.1–4 about the nature and limits of Old Testament sacrifice.

> For since the law has but a shadow of the good things to come

instead of the true form of these realities, it can never, by the same sacrifices that are continually offered every year, make perfect those who draw near. Otherwise, would they not have ceased to be offered, since the worshipers, having once been cleansed, would no longer have any consciousness of sins? But in these sacrifices there is a reminder of sins every year. For it is impossible for the blood of bulls and goats to take away sins.

Now, contrast the limited scope of the millions of Old Testament sacrifices with the once-for-all sacrifice of God's own Son.

But when Christ appeared as a high priest of the good things that have come, then through the greater and more perfect tent (not made with hands, that is, not of this creation) he entered once for all into the holy places, not by means of the blood of goats and calves but by means of his own blood, thus securing an eternal redemption. For if the blood of goats and bulls, and the sprinkling of defiled persons with the ashes of a heifer, sanctify for the purification of the flesh, how much more will the blood of Christ, who through the eternal Spirit offered himself without blemish to God, purify our conscience from dead works to serve the living God. (Heb 9.11–14)

By the shed blood of the Lamb of God and the perfect representation offered by the risen Christ as high priest on our behalf, we can "with confidence draw near to the throne of grace, that we may receive mercy and find grace to help in time of need" (Heb 4.16). Because of our relationship based on promises through Jesus, our Creator is completely merciful toward our iniquities. He remembers our sins no more. Our eternal redemption has been secured by means of the blood of our perfect high priest (Heb 9.12).

Conclusion

The old covenant served a vital purpose in the development of God's plan for the redemption of mankind. For approximately 1,500 years the Mosaic system served as the basis of God's relationship with the descendants of Abraham. But that covenant has been set aside and superseded by a better covenant. Now, all people—Jews and Gentiles—are invited into covenant relationship with God by the sacrifice of his Son. The Lord can change men's minds and renew their hearts. Men can know the Lord and enjoy the forgiveness of their sins.

When we understand this important shift and distinction between the covenants, we recognize that "whatever was written in former days was written for our instruction, that through endurance and through the encouragement of the Scriptures we might have hope" (Rom 15.4). But we do not look to the Old Testament as our guiding authority in matters of worship to God and service to others. It provides a perfect foundation for our understanding of the majesty and need for the better covenant. It was our guardian, our schoolmaster, our tutor until Christ came, in order that we might now be justified by faith. And now that faith has come, we are no longer under that guardian.

> For in Christ Jesus you are all sons of God, through faith. For as many of you as were baptized into Christ have put on Christ. There is neither Jew nor Greek, there is neither slave nor free, there is no male and female, for you are all one in Christ Jesus. And if you are Christ's, then you are Abraham's offspring, heirs according to promise. (Gal 3.23–29)

On this historical side of the cross, our King is Jesus. Our law is the "law of liberty" (Jas 2.12). At this point in God's rescue plan, we are under the scope and authority of the New Testament of Jesus Christ.

Questions for Growth and Discussion

1. When you think of a *covenant*, what do you think of?

2. Are there any other covenants you can remember, particularly from the Old Testament, that human beings made with each other?

3. When God described marriage as a covenant in Malachi 2, there are powerful implications attached. Like what? How

should our marriages be shaped by the recognition that God regards them as a covenant?

4. Is the covenant God made after the flood in Genesis 9 still binding today? Why or why not?

5. What about the covenant he made with Abraham in Genesis 17? Is that still binding today? Why or why not? If not, how should the nation of Israel be regarded today?

6. Circumcision was an undeniable part of God's covenant with Abraham's descendants (Gen 17). How should circumcision be regarded today?

7. Why did God not abandon and obliterate Old Testament Israel for their rebellious negligence?

8. This chapter highlighted Romans 7, 2 Corinthians 3, Galatians 3 and Ephesians 2 as New Testament commentary on God's old covenant with Israel. Can you summarize the basic message of those passages?

9. In what way is the new covenant of Jesus Christ "better" than the old covenant with Israel?

10. What sort of practices and teachings from the Old Testament do modern religious people try to bind or rationalize that are not a part of the new covenant of Christ? What should our response be to such suggestions?

---*four*---

The Bedrock Principle of Authority

AUTHORITY (*noun*) — the power or right to determine, control, command, judge, or prohibit the action of others; dominion; jurisdiction.

We interact with authority every day. We submit ourselves to authority every day. We depend on authority every day. At the gas pump. In the grocery store. When we look at our watches. As we use our money. When we drive our motor vehicles. As we leave the pharmacy.

We expect the fresh fruits and vegetables we buy to meet a certain standard of cleanliness and quality. We take for granted the fact that the prescriptions our pharmacists fill have been regulated and approved by a governing authority. Every single time we cruise beside someone on the highway or fly by another car on a narrow two-way street, we assume that all involved are going to abide by the regulating standards of lawful authority.

Standards of authority have power to teach, reprove, correct and train. When different people with differing ideas and varying histories and conflicting agendas agree to abide under a common standard of authority, unity of mind and purpose is possible. There is potential for peaceful and constructive coexistence. Disagreements can be settled and a clear vision for collective purpose and action in the future can be established.

For instance, if I were to ask you how long this line is…

...what would you say? What would you do? Is there anyone who would disagree that we *can* come to a common understanding of exactly how long that line is? And is there any doubt as to how we would come to agreement? By appealing to a common standard of measuring authority.

God as the Ultimate Authority

With those simple principles in mind, carefully read God's communication to the Israelites in Leviticus 18.1–5.

> And the LORD spoke to Moses, saying, "Speak to the people of Israel and say to them, I am the LORD your God. You shall not do as they do in the land of Egypt, where you lived, and you shall not do as they do in the land of Canaan, to which I am bringing you. You shall not walk in their statutes. You shall follow my rules and keep my statutes and walk in them. I am the LORD your God. You shall therefore keep my statutes and my rules; if a person does them, he shall live by them: I am the LORD."

In Leviticus 19.1–2, he continued,

> "Speak to all the congregation of the people of Israel and say to them, You shall be holy, for I the LORD your God am holy."

It is a principle that is reiterated in the New Testament.

> Therefore, preparing your minds for action, and being sober-minded, set your hope fully on the grace that will be brought to you at the revelation of Jesus Christ. As obedient children, do not be conformed to the passions of your former ignorance, but as he who called you is holy, you also be holy in all your conduct, since it is written, "You shall be holy, for I am holy." (1 Pet 1.13–16)

Why would God act as if he has the right to define, command, prohibit and judge? Why should we feel compelled to be as he is? He is the Creator of all things (Gen 1–2). He is the Giver of all good things (Jas 1.17). He is the Owner of all things (Psa 50.10), including our spirits (Ecc 12.7). Therefore, we ought not be surprised that he presents himself as sovereign and authoritative.

> For my thoughts are not your thoughts,
>> neither are your ways my ways, declares the LORD.
> For as the heavens are higher than the earth,
>> so are my ways higher than your ways
>> and my thoughts than your thoughts. (Isa 55.1–2)

Which means...

My **feelings** and **hunches** and **goals** are not the ultimate standard of authority.

> There is a way that seems right to a man,
>> but its end is the way to death. (Prov 14.12)

My **past personal experiences** are not the ultimate standard of authority.

> Not everyone who says to me, "Lord, Lord," will enter the kingdom of heaven, but the one who does the will of my Father who is in heaven. On that day many will say to me, "Lord, Lord, did we not prophesy in your name, and cast out demons in your name, and do many mighty works in your name?" And then will I declare to them, "I never knew you; depart from me, you workers of lawlessness." (Matt 7.21–23)

My **relatives** are not the ultimate standard of authority.

> Whoever loves father or mother more than me is not worthy of me, and whoever loves son or daughter more than me is not worthy of me. (Matt 10.37)

The **majority** is not the ultimate standard of authority.

> Enter by the narrow gate. For the gate is wide and the way is easy that leads to destruction, and those who enter by it are many. (Matt 7.13)

Religious leaders are not the ultimate standard of authority.

And he said to them, "Well did Isaiah prophesy of you hypocrites, as it is written,

'This people honors me with their lips,
    but their heart is far from me;
in vain do they worship me,
    teaching as doctrines the commandments of men.'

You leave the commandment of God and hold to the tradition of men." (Mark 7.6–8)

My own **conscience** is not the ultimate standard of authority. As Paul confessed,

I myself was convinced that I ought to do many things in opposing the name of Jesus of Nazareth. (Acts 26.9)

God is the ultimate standard of authority.

Concrete Old Testament Examples

A great many examples of men and women who interacted with, submitted themselves to and faithfully depended upon God as the ultimate standard of authority have been preserved for us in the Old Testament. These accounts have been providentially preserved "for our instruction, that through endurance and through the encouragement of the Scriptures we might have hope" (Rom 15.4). For instance,

Noah, in Genesis 6:
    Was given the responsibility by God to build an ark (6.14).
    Did all that God commanded him to do (6.22).
    Was preserved by God (7.23; Heb 11.7).

Abel, in Genesis 4:
    Offered the firstborn of his flock and of their fat portions as a sacrifice to God (4.4).
    Was regarded as offering "a more acceptable sacrifice" to God than Cain (Heb 11.4–5).
    Pleased the LORD (Gen 4.4).

Abraham, in Genesis 12:
> Was told to leave his country and go to the land that God would show him (12.1).
> Obeyed, as the LORD had told him (12.4).
> Was richly blessed and powerfully used by God (Heb 11.12).

But not everyone was willing to submit themselves to God in the Old Testament. Consider a few examples on the other side of the spectrum.

Cain, in Genesis 4:
> Brought to the LORD an offering of the fruit of the ground (4.3).
> Did not "do well" (4.7).
> Did not enjoy the regard of God for his offering and was reproved (4.5–7).

Nadab and Abihu, Leviticus 10:
> Were assigned the task of offering sacrifices to God with "authorized" fire (Exodd 30.9).
> Offered "unauthorized fire before the LORD" (Lev 10.1).
> Were consumed with fire from the LORD (Lev 10.2).

A man gathering sticks, Numbers 15:
> Was to do no work nor kindle a fire on the Sabbath (Exod 20.10; 35.3).
> Gathered sticks on the Sabbath (15.32).
> Was stoned to death by commandment of the LORD (15.35).

In each case, there was some sort of expectation defined by God, there were actions on the part of the people created in his image, and there were consequences of those actions. When these people interacted with God, they were interacting with the ultimate standard of authority. By their actions, they either submitted to God as the ultimate standard of authority, or they did not. Either way, they enjoyed or suffered the consequences of their actions in light of God's authority.

Authority as Established in the New Testament

We clearly discover in Matthew 21.23–27 that the chief priests and elders of the people in Jesus' day appreciated the need for and expected (at least when it suited their purposes) a source of authority to back up human actions.

> And when he entered the temple, the chief priests and the elders of the people came up to him as he was teaching, and said, **"By what authority are you doing these things, and who gave you this authority?"** Jesus answered them, "I also will ask you one question, and if you tell me the answer, then I also will tell you by what authority I do these things. The baptism of John, from where did it come? From heaven or from man?" And they discussed it among themselves, saying, "If we say, 'From heaven,' he will say to us, 'Why then did you not believe him?' But if we say, 'From man,' we are afraid of the crowd, for they all hold that John was a prophet." So they answered Jesus, "We do not know." And he said to them, "Neither will I tell you by what authority I do these things."

Jesus, as he so masterfully did on other occasions, exposed the true condition of their hearts by raising the issue of the baptism of John. "From where did it come?" John needed authority for his actions, but who was the source of that authority? "From heaven?" Did God grant John the authority to preach and do what he was doing, thereby making it legitimate and authoritative? "Or from man?" There can be only two ultimate sources of authority—heaven or human. If heaven, why wouldn't we respond? If human, why couldn't we take it or leave it?

Throughout his ministry, Jesus acted as one who had authority. When he had finished his famous sermon overlooking the Sea of Galilee, "the crowds were astonished at his teaching, for he was teaching as one who had authority, and not as their scribes" (Matt 7.28–29). In Matthew 9.1–8,

> And getting into a boat he crossed over and came to his own city. And behold, some people brought to him a paralytic, lying on a bed. And when Jesus saw their faith, he said to the paralytic,

"Take heart, my son; your sins are forgiven." And behold, some of the scribes said to themselves, "This man is blaspheming." But Jesus, knowing their thoughts, said, "Why do you think evil in your hearts? For which is easier, to say, 'Your sins are forgiven,' or to say, 'Rise and walk'? But that you may know that the Son of Man has authority on earth to forgive sins"—he then said to the paralytic—"Rise, pick up your bed and go home." And he rose and went home. When the crowds saw it, they were afraid, and they glorified God, who had given such authority to men.

But the clearest statement of Jesus concerning his authority was delivered after his resurrection from the dead, prior to his ascension into heaven.

Now the eleven disciples went to Galilee, to the mountain to which Jesus had directed them. And when they saw him they worshiped him, but some doubted. And Jesus came and said to them, "All authority in heaven and on earth has been given to me. Go therefore and make disciples of all nations, baptizing them in the name of the Father and of the Son and of the Holy Spirit, teaching them to observe all that I have commanded you. And behold, I am with you always, to the end of the age." (Matt 28.16–20)

From this point on, these appointed ambassadors of Jesus acted with an important measure of delegated authority. Remember that Jesus had promised they would be guided by the Holy Spirit of God (John 16.7–14; 14.26; 15.26; 17.8, 14). They consistently preached Jesus as their authoritative King and head over the church (Eph 1.22–23), but they also made claims like this:

Therefore, we are ambassadors for Christ, God making his appeal through us. We implore you on behalf of Christ, be reconciled to God. (2 Cor 5.20)

Those who say we need only to give heed to the words of Jesus would do well to remember his charge to his earliest followers in Luke 10.16. "The one who hears you hears me, and the one who rejects you rejects me, and the one who rejects me rejects him who sent me." Conversely, in John 13.20, "Truly, truly, I say to you, whoever receives the one I send receives me, and whoever receives me receives the one who sent me."

In John 20.19–23, Jesus commissioned these specially chosen men with an awesome responsibility.

> On the evening of that day, the first day of the week, the doors being locked where the disciples were for fear of the Jews, Jesus came and stood among them and said to them, "Peace be with you." When he had said this, he showed them his hands and his side. Then the disciples were glad when they saw the Lord. Jesus said to them again, "Peace be with you. As the Father has sent me, even so I am sending you." And when he had said this, he breathed on them and said to them, "Receive the Holy Spirit. If you forgive the sins of any, they are forgiven them; if you withhold forgiveness from any, it is withheld."

Jesus sent the apostles—with authority—just as his Father had sent him. He commanded them, as the source of all authority in heaven and on earth, to make disciples of all nations, baptizing them in the name of the Father and of the Son and of the Holy Spirit, teaching them to observe all that they had received from him.

In Acts 2, Peter, standing with the eleven, lifted up his voice and addressed a great multitude of Jews with authority. Jesus had promised to give "the keys of the kingdom of heaven" in Matthew 16, and those keys were authoritatively used on the Day of Pentecost following Jesus' atoning sacrifice to open the doors of access to God.

> So those who received his word were baptized, and there were added that day about three thousand souls.
>
> And they devoted themselves to the apostles' teaching and the fellowship, to the breaking of bread and the prayers. (Acts 2.41–42)

From this point forward, the apostles' teaching was held as authoritative. They were commissioned envoys of the risen Christ—empowered by the Holy Spirit with "the good news" of

Jesus and verified by incredible miraculous signs (Mark 16.17–18). Wherever they went, they proclaimed "the doctrine of Christ" (2 John 4–9). In the words of the apostle Paul,

> I urge you, then, be imitators of me. That is why I sent you Timothy, my beloved and faithful child in the Lord, to remind you of my ways in Christ, as I teach them everywhere in every church. (1 Cor 4.16–17)

> What you have learned and received and heard and seen in me—practice these things, and the God of peace will be with you. (Phil 4.9)

We interact with heavenly authority as we handle the New Testament. Will we submit ourselves to it? Will we depend upon it?

Questions for Growth and Discussion

1. In your own words, what is authority and why is it important?

2. Take the time to reread God's words in Leviticus 18.1–5 and 19.1–2. What is he saying?

3. Why would God follow up his commandments, prohibitions and promises of judgment with straightforward statements like those that we read in Isaiah 55.1–2?

4. Why are human feelings, hunches and goals an inadequate source of ultimate authority?

5. *Vox populi, vox dei* is a famous ancient Latin phrase that means, "the voice of the people is the voice of God." Why is that not the case?

6. This chapter mentioned three Old Testament examples of people who interacted with, submitted themselves to and faithfully depended upon God as the ultimate standard of authority. Can you think of other Old Testament examples?

7. And what about Old Testament examples of people who were unwilling to submit themselves to God? Can you list a few more examples than were mentioned in this chapter?

8. What were the "keys of the kingdom of heaven" that Jesus promised in Matthew 16?

9. Why is "from heaven or from men" still a valid gauge for modern religious authority and practice?

10. In your own words, what is "the doctrine of Christ" referenced in 2 John 4–9?

five

Of Law and Lawlessness

In the last chapter we briefly referenced Jesus' words in Matthew 7.21–23, but they are worthy of some more in-depth attention at this point.

> Not everyone who says to me, "Lord, Lord," will enter the kingdom of heaven, but the one who does the will of my Father who is in heaven. On that day many will say to me, "Lord, Lord, did we not prophesy in your name, and cast out demons in your name, and do many mighty works in your name?" And then will I declare to them, "I never knew you; depart from me, you workers of lawlessness."

With these words, Jesus established a straightforward distinction between "the will of my Father who is in heaven" and "lawlessness." There are image-bearers of God who do the will of the heavenly Father, and there are image-bearers of God who are workers of lawlessness. The first will gain entrance into the kingdom of heaven, and the latter will be told to depart from God.

It is vital, therefore, that we understand the difference between the will of our Creator and lawlessness.

> Look carefully then how you walk, not as unwise but as wise, making the best use of the time, because the days are evil. Therefore do not be foolish, but understand what the will of the Lord is. (Eph 5.15–17)

In Chapter 2, we established that God's word is profitable for those who "invest" in it. In Chapter 3, we learned that God's will for our lives on this historical side of the cross is revealed in the

New Testament of Jesus Christ. In Chapter 4, we determined that the apostles delivered authoritative teaching as commissioned envoys of the risen Christ (Acts 2.42). What they delivered in oral and written form is to be regarded and abided within as the God-breathed doctrine of Christ (2 John 4–9). We are called to do more than refer to Jesus as "Lord." The one who enters the kingdom of heaven will have put the revealed will of God into practice.

On the other side of the spectrum is "lawlessness." In Greek, the word is *anomia*. *Nomos* in Greek is translated "law" in English. Add an *a* to the front of the word and it makes it negative—similar to the way many of our English words work. A *theist* is someone who believes in God. An *atheist* does not. A *gnostic* is someone who knows. An *agnostic* is someone who does not. *Nomos* is "law." *Anomia* is "lawlessness," or some of our English translations render the Greek word as "iniquity." To be guilty of "lawlessness" is to live outside of the boundaries of the law of God. The people Jesus referenced in Matthew 7 claimed to have done a number of noteworthy things in his name—prophesying, casting out demons and many mighty works. And yet, in spite of their claims, Jesus promised that he will declare, "I never knew you; depart from me, you workers of lawlessness." As we established in Chapter 4, my past personal experiences or achievements are not the ultimate standard of authority.

Our understanding of the Bible's use of "lawlessness" is deepened even further by the writings of John.

> And now, little children, abide in him, so that when he appears we may have confidence and not shrink from him in shame at his coming. If you know that he is righteous, you may be sure that everyone who practices righteousness has been born of him.
>
> See what kind of love the Father has given to us, that we should be called children of God; and so we are. The reason why the world does not know us is that it did not know him. Beloved, we are God's children now, and what we will be has not yet appeared; but we know that when he appears we shall be like him, because we shall see him as he is. And everyone who thus hopes in him purifies himself as he is pure.

Everyone who makes a practice of sinning also practices **lawlessness; sin is lawlessness**. You know that he appeared to take away sins, and in him there is no sin. No one who abides in him keeps on sinning; no one who keeps on sinning has either seen him or known him. Little children, let no one deceive you. Whoever practices righteousness is righteous, as he is righteous. Whoever makes a practice of sinning is of the devil, for the devil has been sinning from the beginning. The reason the Son of God appeared was to destroy the works of the devil. No one born of God makes a practice of sinning, for God's seed abides in him, and he cannot keep on sinning because he has been born of God. By this it is evident who are the children of God, and who are the children of the devil: whoever does not practice righteousness is not of God, nor is the one who does not love his brother. (1 John 2.28–3.10)

It's important to note the significant difference between John's use of the word "lawlessness" in 1 John 3 and his use of the word "abiding" in 2 John 9.

Everyone who **goes on ahead** and **does not abide in the teaching of Christ**, does not have God. Whoever **abides** in the teaching has both the Father and the Son.

To be guilty of "lawlessness" is to live outside of the boundaries of God's law. To "abide in" the teaching of Christ is to live within the boundaries of God's revealed will.

We referenced an Old Testament example of "lawlessness" in Chapter 4.

Now Nadab and Abihu, the sons of Aaron, each took his censer and put fire in it and laid incense on it and offered **unauthorized** fire before the LORD, **which he had not commanded them**. And fire came out from before the LORD and consumed them, and they died before the LORD. (Lev 10.1–2)

Some of our English translations render "unauthorized" as "profane" or "strange," and the implications are clear. The fire that was offered by these two sons of Aaron was "outside of" the boundaries of the law established by God. He had provided a pattern he expected the children of Israel to follow—specific days to remember and keep holy, specific feasts to celebrate in a specific manner, specific animals to sacrifice at specific times, specific individuals to represent the people in specific acts of worship and service in specific ways. When Nadab and Abihu offered fire that was "outside of" the boundaries of the law established by God, it was described by God as "unauthorized," "profane," or "strange."

And so, it's not unusual to find exhortations like that of Moses in Deuteronomy 4.1–2.

> And now, O Israel, listen to the statutes and the rules that I am teaching you, and do them, that you may live, and go in and take possession of the land that the LORD, the God of your fathers, is giving you. **You shall not add to** the word that I command you, **nor take from it,** that you may **keep the commandments** of the LORD your God that I command you.

Clearly, God's people were to have reverent regard for those things which had been authorized by God and for those things which had not.

In the New Testament letter of 2 Thessalonians, the apostle Paul warned first-century Christians that the spirit of "lawlessness" was still alive and well.

> Now concerning the coming of our Lord Jesus Christ and our being gathered together to him, we ask you, brothers, not to be quickly shaken in mind or alarmed, either by a spirit or a spoken word, or a letter seeming to be from us, to the effect that the day of the Lord has come. Let no one deceive you in any way. For that day will not come, unless the rebellion comes first, and the man of **lawlessness** is revealed, the son of destruction, who opposes and exalts himself against every so-called god or object of worship, so that he takes his seat in the temple of God, proclaiming himself to be God. Do you not remember that when I was still with you I told you these things? And you know what is restraining him now so that he

may be revealed in his time. For the mystery of **lawlessness** is already at work. Only he who now restrains it will do so until he is out of the way. And then the **lawless** one will be revealed, whom the Lord Jesus will kill with the breath of his mouth and bring to nothing by the appearance of his coming. The coming of the **lawless** one is by the activity of Satan with all power and false signs and wonders, and with all wicked deception for those who are perishing, because they refused to love the truth and so be saved. Therefore God sends them a strong delusion, so that they may believe what is false, in order that all may be condemned who did not believe the truth but had pleasure in unrighteousness. (2 Thes 2.1–12)

When it comes to our relationship with divine authority, we will either be on the side of law or lawlessness. Passages like 2 Thessalonians 2 make clear what side we should strive to be on.

Other New Testament References to God's Standard of Authority

Take the time to carefully read and reflect on the way the inspired messengers of the New Testament describe the will of God and our responsibility as his children, beginning with the words of Jesus.

The one who rejects me and does not receive my words has a judge; **the word that I have spoken** will judge him on the last day. For I have not spoken on my own authority, but the Father who sent me has himself given me a commandment—what to say and what to speak. And I know that his commandment is eternal life. What I say, therefore, I say as the Father has told me. (John 12.48–50)

But thanks be to God, that you who were once slaves of sin have become obedient from the heart to **the standard of teaching** to which you were committed, and, having been set free from sin, have become slaves of righteousness. (Rom 6.17–18)

Now we have received not the spirit of the world, but the Spirit who is from God, that we might understand the things freely given us by God. And we impart this in words not taught by human wisdom but taught by the Spirit, interpreting **spiritual truths** to those who are spiritual. (1 Cor 2.12–13)

I have applied all these things to myself and Apollos for your benefit, brothers, that you may learn by us **not to go beyond what is written**, that none of you may be puffed up in favor of one against another. For who sees anything different in you? What do you have that you did not receive? If then you received it, why do you boast as if you did not receive it? (1 Cor 4.6–7)

Or was it from you that the word of God came? Or are you the only ones it has reached? If anyone thinks that he is a prophet, or spiritual, he should acknowledge that the things I am writing to you are **a command of the Lord**. If anyone does not recognize this, he is not recognized. (1 Cor 14.36–38)

I am astonished that you are so quickly deserting him who called you in the grace of Christ and are turning to **a different gospel—not that there is another one**, but there are some who trouble you and want to distort the gospel of Christ. But even if we or an angel from heaven should preach to you a gospel contrary to the one we preached to you, let him be accursed. As we have said before, so now I say again: If anyone is preaching to you a gospel contrary to the one you received, let him be accursed. (Gal 1.6–9)

Follow **the pattern of the sound words** that you have heard from me, in the faith and love that are in Christ Jesus. By the Holy Spirit who dwells within us, guard the good deposit entrusted to you. (2 Tim 1.13–14)

You then, my child, be strengthened by the grace that is in Christ Jesus, and **what you have heard from me** in the presence of many witnesses entrust to faithful men who will be able to teach others also. (2 Tim 2.1–2)

But be doers of the word, and not hearers only, deceiving yourselves. For if anyone is a hearer of the word and not a doer, he is like a man who looks intently at his natural face in a mirror. For he looks at himself and goes away and at once forgets what he was like. But the one who looks into **the perfect law, the law of**

liberty, and perseveres, being no hearer who forgets but a doer who acts, he will be blessed in his doing. (Jas 1.22–25)

As each has received a gift, use it to serve one another, as good stewards of God's varied grace: whoever speaks, as one who speaks **oracles of God**; whoever serves, as one who serves by the strength that God supplies—in order that in everything God may be glorified through Jesus Christ. To him belong glory and dominion forever and ever. Amen. (1 Pet 4.10–11)

Beloved, although I was very eager to write to you about our common salvation, I found it necessary to write appealing to you to contend for **the faith** that was once for all delivered to the saints. (Jude 3)

I warn everyone who hears the words of the prophecy of this book: **if anyone adds to** them, God will add to him the plagues described in this book, and **if anyone takes away from** the words of the book of this prophecy, God will take away his share in the tree of life and in the holy city, which are described in this book. (Rev 22.18–19)

When God's people are willing to submit themselves to God's revealed will and abide within the teaching God has provided, God's people can enjoy unity of mind and action.

I appeal to you, brothers, by the name of our Lord Jesus Christ, that **all of you agree**, and that there be **no divisions among you**, but that you be **united in the same mind** and **the same judgment**. (1 Cor 1.10)

Walk as **children of light** (for the fruit of light is found in all that is good and right and true), and try to discern what is pleasing to the Lord. (Eph 5.8–10)

Nevertheless, to the degree that we have already attained, let us walk by **the same rule**, let us be of **the same mind**. Brethren, join in following my example, and note those who so walk, as you have us for **a pattern**. (Phil 3.16–17, NKJV)

Let the word of Christ dwell in you richly, teaching and admonishing one another in all wisdom, singing psalms and hymns and spiritual songs, with thankfulness in your hearts to God. And whatever you do, in word or deed, **do everything in the name of the Lord Jesus,** giving thanks to God the Father through him. (Col 3.16–17)

Do not despise prophecies, but **test everything; hold fast what is good.** Abstain from every form of evil. (1 Thess 5.20–22)

There is a Lord over all humanity. This Lord has a will. His will can be understood. To live in willful ignorance of or rebellion against the will of the Lord is lawlessness. And one day we will all give account for the way we have lived in relation to his will.

Just as the weeds are gathered and burned with fire, so will it be at the close of the age. The Son of Man will send his angels, and they will gather out of his kingdom **all causes of sin** and **all law-breakers,** and throw them into the fiery furnace. In that place there will be weeping and gnashing of teeth. Then the righteous will shine like the sun in the kingdom of their Father. He who has ears, let him hear. (Matt 13.30–33)

Therefore, the words of God to Cain thousands of years ago still ring true.

If you do well, will you not be accepted? And if you do not do well, sin is crouching at the door. Its desire is for you, but you must rule over it. (Gen 4.7)

So speak and so act as those who are to be judged under the law of liberty. (Jas 2.12)

Questions for Growth and Discussion

1. In your own words, describe "lawlessness." Can you illustrate it using a modern analogy?

2. In 1 John 2.28, we are encouraged as little children to "abide in him, so that when he appears we may have confidence and not shrink from him in shame at his coming." What does it mean, practically speaking, to "abide in" Jesus?

3. In your own words, what is the Spirit of God communicating in 1 John 3.6?

4. Why would John say that "whoever makes a practice of sinning is of the devil" (1 John 3.8)?

5. Carefully reread 2 John 9. What is "the teaching of Christ" and what does it mean to "abide in it"? In what way will the abider "have" both the Father and the Son?

6. What should we make of Paul's dark words in 2 Thessalonians 2.1–12?

7. In 2 Timothy 1.13, Paul encouraged Timothy to "follow the pattern of sound words" that he had received. What is a "pattern," and in what way does God's word serve as a "pattern"? What are "sound" words?

8. What did James have in mind when he writes of "the perfect law, the law of liberty" (Jas 1.25)? In what way is the law that we as Christians are under a law of "liberty" (Jas 2.12)?

9. What did Peter have in mind when he referenced "the oracles of God" in 1 Peter 4.11?

10. What was "the faith" for which Jude encouraged Christians to contend in Jude 3?

six

Context, Context, Context

If you've ever tried to buy or sell a house, you've probably heard the most popular mantra in real estate: "Location, location, location." It simply means that identical houses can increase or decrease in value due to their physical location. It's the number one rule in real estate, and it's often the most overlooked.

The same sort of thing could be said about our efforts to interpret the Bible: "Location, location, location." Or, another way of putting it is: "Context, context, context." Edwin Crozier illustrates this principle by sharing the opening paragraph of a book entitled *Murder at Cory Mansion*.

> A few minutes of stillness lingered at the Cory Mansion, when the night sounds were shattered by a woman's scream and an infant's cry. A few minutes later, as the clock in the hall struck 2:30, a man carrying a black leather handbag slipped quickly from the house, glanced up and down the street, and walked briskly away through the early morning mist.

What happened? Someone was clearly robbed and murdered in the middle of the night. Sadly, this someone probably had an infant. We certainly hope the sleuth in this mystery catches the bad guy.

The truth is, Edwin made the book and its opening paragraph up to illustrate a simple point. Look again at the same paragraph, but read it this time as the opening paragraph to a book entitled, *The Life and Times of Richard Cory*.

With that title, the opening paragraph has a completely different meaning, doesn't it? Instead of describing a murder, it describes the birth of a new baby. Instead of a murderer fleeing the crime scene, we can easily envision a doctor leaving a wealthy patient's home, hurrying to rest before the next morning's work.

What changed? We read the exact same paragraph in both situations. But in each case, we **interpreted** the paragraph's meaning differently. Why? In each case, we were reading a different *kind* of book. We took into account the genre of writing. One was a mystery, the other a biographical narrative.

And that leads us to the point of this section of our study. In previous chapters we've noted the Bible is precious and profitable. We've investigated the bedrock principle of authority and how we will either operate within the boundaries of law or be guilty of lawlessness. We've established the importance of distinguishing between the covenants of the Bible. In this lesson, we focus on the importance of distinguishing between the different genres that God used in his written revelation to mankind.

Gen-What?

From Genesis to Revelation, we run across different types of literature. In other words, the Bible isn't written in the same way from cover to cover. Almighty God saw fit to use different genres at different points in his progressive revelation. A *genre* is simply a category or class of communicating that uses specific styles or forms. This point is vital to understand because if we read every part of the Bible in the same way, we're going to misunderstand and misapply the Scriptures. It doesn't take long to notice the Psalms don't read or sound the same as the prophecy of Isaiah. Isaiah reads and sounds different than the Gospel of Matthew. We don't learn the same things in the same ways from Jesus' parable of the sower as we do the historical account of Noah in Genesis 6.

Perhaps you've heard the illustration of the man who randomly opened his Bible to Matthew 27.5—the account where Judas threw the betrayal money into the temple, departed, and hanged himself. The careless reader then haphazardly landed in Luke 10.37—Jesus' encouragement to "go, and do likewise." The reader frantically began flipping pages and his eyes came to rest on John 13.27—"What you are going to do, do quickly." He was nearly pushed over the edge when he fearfully and sloppily turned to Acts 22.16, only to find the question, "And now why do you wait?"

It's all right there in the Bible! But clearly, *how* we read the Bible matters. Context, context, context is everything! God used different kinds of communication at different points in history to different audiences in accordance with a perfectly executed plan to convey his unified message of redemption to mankind. Appreciating those facts is an indispensable aspect of "accurately handling" the word of truth (2 Tim 2.15).

Categories of Biblical Communication

Prose. We are most used to reading this "normal," matter-of-fact, straightforward type of communication. When it comes to prose, the author typically means what he says and says what he means. While figures of speech can appear in prose, they rarely cause us any problems because they're obvious. When Paul wrote in Ephesians 4.28, "Let the thief no longer steal," we don't look for hidden or symbolic meaning. We take it at face value—followers of Jesus must not steal. That's prose.

Narrative. This form of prose tells a story. It documents the thoughts, actions, events, and circumstances of people. Narrative, as a form of prose, is straightforward. We don't typically look for hidden and symbolic meanings in narrative. But when it comes to the narrative accounts of the Bible, we're looking to do more than simply read the historical information. When we read about Cain and Abel in Genesis 4.1–8, we don't wonder what Cain and Abel represent, nor do we question what the sheep and the vegetables symbolize. Cain represents Cain and his vegetables are just that—vegetables. The same is true for Abel and his sheep.

But we *can* learn more than just historical facts in the narrative accounts of the Bible. In cases like that of Cain and Abel, we can discern principles for how *we* ought to live in relation to God. We learn that we must do things God's way. We learn that God cares about what we do and how we react. We learn that we mustn't murder. If we read this story just like the prose of Ephesians 4.28, we would learn what happened between Cain and Abel, but we wouldn't learn practical principles of application. We must consider the genre.

Poetry. This is where things begin to get a little tricky for most of us. Hebrew poetry doesn't necessarily rely on rhyming sounds and metrical reading like classical English poetry. Rather, Hebrew poetry often relies on what some have called "rhyming thoughts." Consider Psalm 3.1–4:

> O LORD, how many are my foes!
> > Many are rising against me;
> many are saying of my soul,
> > there is no salvation for him in God.
>
> But you, O LORD, are a shield about me,
> > my glory, and the lifter of my head.
> I cried aloud to the LORD,
> > and he answered me from his holy hill.

The words don't rhyme (for one, they're translated from Hebrew into English), but the content is parallel. The first two verses focus on David's foes; the second two focus on David's God. There are many foes, but God is a shield. Many are rising against David, but God is his glory. Many are slandering the soul of David, but God is the lifter of his head.

One difficulty we frequently have with Biblical poetry is that it's often highly figurative and symbolic. When we read it, we get the sense that we shouldn't take everything at literal face value. We have to consider a deeper meaning than what is right there on the surface. For instance, take David's plea to God in Psalm 51.7–8:

> Purge me with hyssop, and I shall be clean;
> > wash me, and I shall be whiter than snow.
> Let me hear joy and gladness;
> > let the bones that you have broken rejoice.

We know David isn't saying that all he needs is for God to rub a hyssop branch all over him. David is employing the imagery of a Jewish priest who would make a defiled house clean by using a hyssop branch that had been dipped in the blood of a sacrifice (Num 19.14–22). David feels the intense need to be cleansed of sin's defilement and he uses highly figurative language to poetically express that need to God. We can also deduce that David isn't talking about bones God had literally broken. Instead, David is expressing his profound guilt in very vivid and painful terms. The point? If we read poetry the same way we read prose or narrative—or vice versa—we will misunderstand the meaning of significant Bible passages.

Proverb. Of course, this genre is used most frequently in the Old Testament book of Proverbs. However, there are proverbs in other places as well (i.e. Ezek 18.2). Proverbs are often poetical, using couplets and rhyming ideas to make their point. But the reason we need to view these as a separate genre is because proverbs are rarely to be read as absolutes. Typically, they are wise maxims—general truths that contain weighty advice. Therefore, while Proverbs 15.1 reads,

A soft answer turns away wrath,
    but a harsh word stirs up anger.

…we don't accuse God of lying when we're dealing with someone who is irrationally irate and constantly angry with us, regardless of how softly we speak to him. The same point applies to Proverbs 22.6:

Train up a child in the way he should go;
    even when he is old he will not depart from it.

If an adult child chooses to turn away from the Biblical instruction he or she consistently and lovingly received from his or her parents, we don't abandon the Bible as a book of lies and false promises. Proverbs 22.6 is a wise maxim—a general truth that contains weighty advice.

Parables. Like narrative, this form of writing tells a story. And yet, while narrative is simply about whatever happened, parables are designed to convey spiritual meaning beyond what is actually written. When we read narrative, we don't have to wonder what objects and people represent. In parables, we do. In Matthew 13.3–9, Jesus told the parable of the sower, and he even clarified its much deeper meaning in Matthew 13.18–23. His words had a much more profound point than a simple observation about different kinds of ground. It was a commentary, warning, and encouragement about the differing conditions of the human heart and its receptiveness to the gospel.

Sometimes the Bible explains the deeper meaning of parables in detail; sometimes we simply read the parables and depend upon further study to discern the deeper meaning (e.g. Luke 16.1–12). But if we read parables just like narratives, we'll be left wondering, "What does this have to do with anything?" If we read narratives like parables, we'll over-spiritualize everything and come up with significantly unfounded ideas.

Prophecy. In general terms, prophecies are communications from a spokesman about things that have not yet happened but will happen at some point in the future. Some prophecies in the Bible were written in a very straightforward manner. They foretold that something was going to happen and even elaborated with details. Consider God's promise in Joel 2.28–29.

> And it shall come to pass afterward,
>   that I will pour out my Spirit on all flesh;
> your sons and your daughters shall prophesy,
>   your old men shall dream dreams,
>   and your young men shall see visions.
> Even on the male and female servants
>   in those days I will pour out my Spirit.

On the other hand, some prophecies were highly symbolic, using past history and iconic images to describe future events. Consider Isaiah 2.2–3, which uses common Jewish imagery to describe the coming kingdom of the Christ which would be established more than 700 years later.

> It shall come to pass in the latter days
>   that the mountain of the house of the LORD

shall be established as the highest of the mountains,
and shall be lifted up above the hills;
and all the nations shall flow to it,
and many peoples shall come, and say:
"Come, let us go up to the mountain of the LORD,
to the house of the God of Jacob,
that he may teach us his ways
and that we may walk in his paths."
For out of Zion shall go the law,
and the word of the LORD from Jerusalem.

Not all prophecy was limited to the Old Testament. "Destroy this temple, and in three days I will raise it up" (John 2.19). Jesus used the temple in Jerusalem as a figure to prophetically foretell his own death and resurrection.

Another device often used in prophecy is what is frequently referred to as "prophetic certainty." God, wanting his people to know how certain his promises for the future were, sometimes spoke of them as if they had already occurred. Isaiah 53 spoke of the coming Messiah as if he had already lived and died. However, this was written 700 years before Jesus walked the earth.

There is much more that could be said about prophecy. But, fundamentally, we need to realize we don't read prophecy like we read narrative, prose, poetry or parable. If we do, we're bound to misunderstand and misapply the Scriptures.

Apocalyptic. While we are typically unfamiliar with this kind of writing, it wasn't foreign to the ancient Hebrews and Christians. They didn't have as much trouble as we do with books like Ezekiel, Zechariah and Revelation because they had read other books written in the same style. Apocalyptic literature was often employed during times of great stress and duress in the ancient world. For Jews of the Old Testament and Christians of the New, apocalyptic language was used as a highly symbolic and exciting way to explain that, in the end, God was going to win and win big. That's the main point behind every apocalyptic book of the Bible—no matter how bad things look, God wins and you want to be on his side.

In some ways, reading their ancient apocalyptic literature is like watching one of our movies. As we watch an old Western, when we see a cowboy in a white hat, we automatically know he's a good guy. The point of nearly all Westerns is that you want to be a good guy, because, in the end, the good guys win. We don't spend an inordinate amount of time wondering what the horses symbolize or why the tumbleweeds blew across the road at the angle they did. We don't wonder why the hero fired ten shots from a six-shot pistol. We naturally take the picture in as a whole. We don't break it down into its tiniest parts and insist on figuring out a meaning for each detail.

In the same way, consider Ezekiel 1. As we read of Ezekiel's incredible vision by the River Chebar, we should guard against missing the overall point because of an excessive fixation on the various faces and wings and colors and wheels. The intensely graphic language is used to overwhelmingly convey the awesome, powerful, glorious nature of the Lord (Ezek 1.28).

Apocalyptic literature also frequently uses numbers in a highly symbolic and figurative way. In Daniel 9, for instance, when the angel Gabriel told Daniel about 70 weeks in which God was going to accomplish several amazing parts of his plan, we shouldn't expect to find fulfillment in 70 literal weeks. Nor do we have to come up with some arbitrary "a-day-equals-a-year-theory" to make the number seem literal. Instead, we note that 70 is the combination of two numbers that often represented fullness and completeness in the ancient world (7 and 10). Thus, Gabriel was communicating to Daniel that God would accomplish all these things when the time was right.

Obviously, we don't have the time or the space to go over every aspect of the symbolism of apocalyptic literature, but what we *can* see is we should avoid reading these writings in the same way that we read poetry, parable or prose. We need to read it as its own genre; otherwise, we're going to misunderstand and misapply it.

Some Simple Guidelines for Honest Bible Study

Appreciate and keep scriptures in their context. Taking something "in context" literally means to take it "with text." That is, we determine a statement's meaning based on the text around it. Psalm 14.1 plainly reads, "There is no God," but it has a context that needs to be noted! Take the time to read (at the very least) the paragraph before and after a specific statement in the Bible to accurately appreciate its intended meaning.

Beyond the immediate context, continue to grow in your grasp of the **overall** context of God's word. What has he revealed about this matter in other portions of the Bible? "**All** Scripture is breathed out by God" (2 Tim 3.16–17). If my interpretation of one passage in God's book contradicts another passage in God's book, the problem is not with God's book but with my interpretation. As the psalmist wrote in Psalm 119.160, "The **sum** of your word is truth."

More people worldwide know John 3.16 than any other verse in the Bible. Many have based their entire understanding of God's nature and mankind's salvation on this one verse. However, God has said much more in his book about love (1 Cor 13.4–7; 1 John 4) and faith (Heb 11; James 2) than the one sentence in John 3.16. Those passages don't contradict John 3.16, but they profoundly deepen our understanding of what Jesus meant in John 3.16. We desperately need to discover and apply what God has revealed about the multiple aspects of his character (Rom 11.22) and the elements of our response to his offer of grace (Rom 10.9–10; Acts 2.38). The sum of God's word is truth.

Grow in your appreciation of the harmony of the Scriptures. In 2 Corinthians 1.17–18, Paul wanted to make sure that Christians understood a foundational principle.

> Was I vacillating when I wanted to do this? Do I make my plans according to the flesh, ready to say "Yes, yes" and "No, no" at the same time? As surely as God is faithful, our word to you has not been Yes and No.

In 1 Corinthians 4.17, he asserted that he taught the same

ways of Christ everywhere in every church. God's message—regardless of who is speaking and to whom it is being spoken—is consistent, unified, and harmonious. Again, if my understanding of one passage contradicts my understanding of another, it is I who is somewhere mistaken.

I need to be careful, therefore, about jumping to shallow interpretations of any passage of Scripture without harmonizing it with everything I know about other statements in God's book. My understanding of John 3.16 must harmonize with passages like Romans 10.9–10 and Acts 2.38. One passage says we need to believe. Another says we need to believe and confess. Yet another says we need to repent and be baptized for the remission of our sins. If I use one passage against the others, I'm missing the point. My understanding should be shaped by a harmony of everything God has said on the matter. When I understand that the faith Jesus describes in John 3.16 is not just "mental assent" but true conviction that produces a response, I can discern the natural place of confession, repentance, and baptism. The sum of God's word is truth.

Allow the simple to define and clarify the complex. Learning God's will to the best of my ability is an ongoing process that involves progressive growth.

> So put away all malice and all deceit and hypocrisy and envy and all slander. Like newborn infants, long for the pure spiritual milk, that by it you may grow up into salvation— if indeed you have tasted that the Lord is good. (1 Pet 2.1–3)

> For though by this time you ought to be teachers, you need someone to teach you again the basic principles of the oracles of God. You need milk, not solid food, for everyone who lives on milk is unskilled in the word of righteousness, since he is a child. But solid food is for the mature, for those who have their powers of discernment trained by constant practice to distinguish good from evil.

> Therefore let us leave the elementary doctrine of Christ and go on to maturity, not laying again a foundation of repentance from dead works and of faith toward God, and of instruction about washings, the laying on of hands, the resur-

rection of the dead, and eternal judgment. And this we will do if God permits. (Heb 5.12–6.3)

There is nothing wrong and everything right with working from the simple and shallow toward the complex and deep. That being the case, let's remember that the complex and deep issues of Scripture will never come back to rewrite the foundational principles of the faith.

As even the apostle Peter wrote in 2 Peter 3.15–16, there are some passages of Scripture that are "hard to understand, which the ignorant and unstable twist to their own destruction." While the exact meaning of some verses or chapters may continue to be debated, we can be steadfastly certain of what they *cannot* mean because of some of the simpler, more straightforward statements in God's book.

For instance, Revelation 20.4 speaks of martyred saints reigning with Christ for a thousand years. I have some strong ideas regarding what that passage means. However, I'm not convinced I flawlessly understand this verse or even the entire chapter. And yet, at the same time, I'm absolutely convinced of some things Revelation 20 *cannot* be saying. It can't be saying that Jesus is coming to the earth some time in our future to establish an earthly kingdom. Why? Other simpler, more straightforward passages forbid that interpretation.

In John 18.36, Jesus said his kingdom was not of this world.

In Mark 9.1 he said some who were standing there would not "taste death" until they saw "the kingdom of God" after it had come with power.

Colossians 1.13 says Christians are already delivered into Christ's kingdom.

In Revelation 1.9, John indicates he and his readers were companions in the kingdom.

Why, then, would he say in Revelation 20 the kingdom would be established thousands of years later? His words must mean something else. We certainly continue to study Revelation 20, but allowing the simple to define the complex helps us to narrow the path a great deal.

We must remember that we are always growing. Some Bible students come across difficult passages and decide that if they don't understand them, there must be no understanding them. They leave the faith, claiming the Bible can't be trusted. If we're still growing, as 2 Peter 1.5–11 demonstrates we must be, then we're going to find issues that are hard to understand. So we simply keep studying God's word. The greater the foundation we progressively develop, the greater the potential for eventual answers to our questions. If we ever forget we're growing, we close ourselves off to the growth, correction and discipline God's word can provide.

When you pick up your Bible, do your best to read it with eager eyes, a willing attitude and a receptive heart. Approach it with the posture of a student who is anxious to grow in his understanding, be corrected in his misconceptions, and galvanized in his convictions.

Questions for Growth and Discussion

1. In your own words, what is "context" and why is keeping God's written revelation in its appropriate context so vital to sound interpretation?

2. In 2 Timothy 2.15, Paul encouraged young Timothy: "Do your best to present yourself to God as one approved, a worker who has no need to be ashamed, rightly handling the word of truth." Are there any aspects of that encouragement that apply to us today? If so, what are they, and how can we step up to meet them?

3. Find two or three examples of **prose** in the Scriptures and summarize—in your own words—what prose is.

4. Find two or three examples of **narrative** in the Scriptures and summarize—in your own words—what narrative is.

5. Find two or three examples of **poetry** in the Scriptures and summarize—in your own words—what poetry is.

6. Find two or three examples of **proverbs** in the Scriptures and summarize—in your own words—what proverbs are.

7. Find two or three examples of **parables** in the Scriptures and summarize—in your own words—what parables are.

8. Find two or three examples of **prophecy** in the Scriptures and summarize—in your own words—what prophecy is.

9. Find two or three examples of **apocalyptic language** in the Scriptures and summarize—in your own words—what apocalyptic language is.

10. Can you give an example or two of a section or principle of Scripture where it has been helpful for you to allow the simple to define and clarify the complex?

seven

How Does the Bible Direct Us?

Consider the foundation we've methodically laid thus far in our guide to Bible study. The goal has been to start at basic "ground-level" and gradually build, one layer of understanding upon another.

The Bible is the world's most precious book.

All Scripture is breathed out by God and profitable for those who invest in it.

The old law of Moses served a vital role in God's eternal plan, but, on this historical side of the cross, we live under the scope of the new covenant of Jesus Christ.

There are two ultimate sources of authority—heavenly and human. As we handle the New Testament, we're interacting with heavenly authority.

Based on our ongoing interaction with this heavenly authority, we will function either on the side of "law" or "lawlessness." We are encouraged by the Spirit of God to speak and to act as those who will be "judged under the law of liberty" (Jas 2.12).

We must appreciate the contexts of differing Biblical genres if we are to "accurately handle the word of truth" (2 Tim 2.15).

But how, practically speaking, does the Bible direct us? In

real-life terms, how do we transition from reading God-breathed words on the printed pages of our Bibles to leading God-approved lives in our own modern contexts? How can I faithfully interpret his communication to mankind that was delivered thousands of years ago and faithfully apply it to my own individual life? How does God speak to *me* and direct *me* at this point in history? Consider six "connective paths" between the word of God and the human heart.

Straightforward Declarations of Truth

There are hundreds, if not thousands, of straightforward, direct, to-the-point statements throughout both the Old and New Testaments. They are candidly delivered truths from divinely-appointed spokesmen, Spirit-led writers, or, at times, even from the very mouth of God himself. From the eternal mind of the infinite Creator, these matter-of-fact statements of truth are communicated to finite, temporal human beings so that we, as image-bearers of God, might believe and act upon his will for our lives. Examples of this "connective path" between the word of God and the human heart abound.

In the beginning, God created the heavens and the earth. (Gen 1.1)

For my thoughts are not your thoughts,
neither are your ways my ways, declares the LORD.
For as the heavens are higher than the earth,
so are my ways higher than your ways
and my thoughts than your thoughts. (Isa 55.8–9)

For God will bring every deed into judgment, with every secret thing, whether good or evil. (Ecc 12.14)

In the beginning was the Word, and the Word was with God, and the Word was God... And the Word became flesh and dwelt among us, and we have seen his glory, glory as of the only Son from the Father, full of grace and truth. (John 1.1, 14)

I am not ashamed of the gospel, for it is the power of God for salvation to everyone who believes, to the Jew first and also to the Greek. For in it the righteousness of God is revealed from faith for faith, as it is written, "The righteous shall live by faith." (Rom 1.16–17)

Blessed be the God and Father of our Lord Jesus Christ, who has blessed us in Christ with every spiritual blessing in the heavenly places, even as he chose us in him before the foundation of the world, that we should be holy and blameless before him. In love he predestined us for adoption as sons through Jesus Christ, according to the purpose of his will, to the praise of his glorious grace, with which he has blessed us in the Beloved. (Eph 1.3–6)

He who testifies to these things says, "Surely I am coming soon." (Rev 22.20)

Regardless of my reaction, these are straightforward declarations of truth from the Creator of the universe to humanity. I can hear them, believe them, and act upon them or not, but my ignorance of or chafing under or rebelling against these God-breathed truths will not change the fact that they are true. God has seen fit to define reality for all mankind in a written revelation. As a part of that revelation, he makes many straightforward declarations of truth.

Overarching Principles

A *principle* is a general law or basic truth from which further elements of instruction or expectation are derived. Principles provide a guiding sense of requirement and obligation. They serve as the groundwork of a system, an essential part of a whole. Jesus' words in Matthew 6.22–24 are just a few of the many principles we find in the New Testament. Like foundational building blocks, they support the superstructure of Christian living.

The eye is the lamp of the body. So, if your eye is healthy, your whole body will be full of light, but if your eye is bad, your whole body will be full of darkness. If then the light in you is darkness, how great is the darkness!

> No one can serve two masters, for either he will hate the one and love the other, or he will be devoted to the one and despise the other. You cannot serve God and money.

There's a difference between "In the beginning, God created the heavens and the earth" and "You cannot serve God and money." The former is a straightforward declaration of truth; the latter is an overarching principle. It's not a specific command or an explicit example, but it *is* an overarching principle. Regardless of my geographical, historical or cultural context, the overarching principle holds true—I cannot simultaneously serve God and money.

Or consider another example from Matthew 10.37–42.

> Whoever loves father or mother more than me is not worthy of me, and whoever loves son or daughter more than me is not worthy of me. And whoever does not take his cross and follow me is not worthy of me. Whoever finds his life will lose it, and whoever loses his life for my sake will find it.
>
> Whoever receives you receives me, and whoever receives me receives him who sent me. The one who receives a prophet because he is a prophet will receive a prophet's reward, and the one who receives a righteous person because he is a righteous person will receive a righteous person's reward. And whoever gives one of these little ones even a cup of cold water because he is a disciple, truly, I say to you, he will by no means lose his reward.

Strictly speaking, there is no "command" in these words of Jesus. And yet, there are several overarching principles that all disciples of Christ must respect. My relationship with Jesus takes precedence over any and all earthly relationships. I must die to self and live for him. The disciple who selflessly shows compassion to others will be rewarded by the Lord.

Or consider the admonition of Paul in 2 Corinthians 9.6–7.

> The point is this: whoever sows sparingly will also reap sparingly, and whoever sows bountifully will also reap bountifully. Each one must give as he has decided in his heart, not reluctantly or under compulsion, for God loves a cheerful giver.

With these two sentences, Paul delivered so much more than a command to give. The Spirit of God, through Paul, established an overarching principle for God's people. Whether I'm a Jew or a Gentile, when I give of my resources, I'm to give from the heart. Whether I'm a man or a woman, if I adhere to the command to give but do so with a selfishly reluctant and grudging heart, I haven't met the Lord's expectations for my life. Why? Because there are overarching principles that apply to my life as a created, redeemed child of God. Regardless of the geographical, historical or cultural context, God loves a *cheerful* giver.

Overarching principles with divine implications for human application are all over the New Testament. From the description of the church as a body with many members (1 Cor 12.12–31) to the more excellent way of love (1 Cor 13), from the armor of God (Eph 6.10–20) to Paul's illustrations of soldiers, athletes, and farmers (2 Tim 2.4–7), God deepens our understanding of his will via the connective path of overarching principles.

Affirmative Commands

In Luke 6.46, Jesus asked, "Why do you call me, 'Lord, Lord,' and not do what I tell you?" Walking with Christ involves not only avoiding that which is evil (more on that in a moment), but also actively doing and involving myself in that which is good. If the Son of God or one of his commissioned envoys tells me to do something, I must do it! I am under the jurisdiction of the One who has "all authority in heaven and on earth." His inspired messengers—whose God-directed work I have in the form of the New Testament—were authoritatively instructed to "go and make disciples of all nations, baptizing them in the name of the Father and of the Son and of the Holy Spirit, teaching them to observe all that I have commanded you" (Matt 28.18–20). They said things like, "If anyone thinks that he is a prophet, or spiritual, he should acknowledge that the things I am writing to you are a command of the Lord" (1 Cor 14.37). Many of those commands were to affirmatively *do* something. Consider the positive commands in Romans 12.

Let love be genuine (12.9)
Abhor what is evil (12.9)
Hold fast to what is good (12.9)
Love one another with brotherly affection (12.10)
Outdo one another in showing honor (12.10)
Be fervent in spirit (12.11)
Serve the Lord (12.11)
Rejoice in hope (12.12)
Be patient in tribulation (12.12)
Be constant in prayer (12.12)
Contribute to the needs of the saints (12.13)
Seek to show hospitality (12.13)
Bless those who persecute you (12.14)
Rejoice with those who rejoice (12.15)
Weep with those who weep (12.15)
Live in harmony with one another (12.16)
Associate with the lowly (12.16)
Give thought to do what is honorable in the sight of all (12.17)
If possible, so far as it depends on you, live peaceably with all (12.18)
If your enemy is hungry, feed him; if he is thirsty, give him something to drink (12.20)
Overcome evil with good (12.21)

The very first gospel invitation was founded on an affirmative command—"Repent and be baptized every one of you in the name of Jesus Christ for the forgiveness of your sins, and you will receive the gift of the Holy Spirit" (Acts 2.38). The examples are all over the New Testament. One of the methods God uses to communicate his will for our lives is affirmative commands. "Do this!"

Negative Prohibitions

On the other hand, just as God has clearly told us to *do* some things, he has authoritatively *prohibited* us from doing other things. Returning to the same context of Romans 12:

Do not be slothful in zeal (12.11)
Do not curse those who persecute you (12.14)
Do not be haughty (12.16)
Never be wise in your own sight (12.16)
Repay no one evil for evil (12.17)
Never avenge yourselves (12.19)
Do not be overcome by evil (12.21)

As our Father in heaven who is good and does good (Psa 119.68), he is seeking to mold us and discipline us *for* our good.

> For what son is there whom his father does not discipline? If you are left without discipline, in which all have participated, then you are illegitimate children and not sons. Besides this, we have had earthly fathers who disciplined us and we respected them. Shall we not much more be subject to the Father of spirits and live? For they disciplined us for a short time as it seemed best to them, but **he disciplines us for our good, that we may share his holiness.** For the moment all discipline seems painful rather than pleasant, but later it yields the peaceful fruit of righteousness to those who have been trained by it. (Heb 12.7–11)

Our responsibility, "as obedient children," is to avoid conformity "to the passions" of our "former ignorance, but as he who called you is holy, you also be holy in all your conduct, since it is written, 'You shall be holy, for I am holy'" (1 Pet 1.14–16). Our heavenly Father defines and describes and warns against that which is unholy via the connective path of negative prohibitions. He says "Don't do that!" many times in his revelation to mankind.

Positive and Negative Examples

Jesus Christ commissioned his apostles with authority. He drew lines in the sand when he said things like, "The one who hears you hears me, and the one who rejects you rejects me, and the one who rejects me rejects him who sent me" (Luke 10.16). On this basis the apostle Paul called attention to his own example.

I urge you, then, **be imitators of me**. That is why I sent you Timothy, my beloved and faithful child in the Lord, to remind you of my ways in Christ, **as I teach them everywhere in every church**. (1 Cor 4.16–17)

What you have learned and received and heard and seen in me—**practice these things**, and the God of peace will be with you. (Phil 4.9)

Follow **the pattern of the sound words** that you have heard from me, in the faith and love that are in Christ Jesus. (2 Tim 1.13)

You then, my child, be strengthened by the grace that is in Christ Jesus, and **what you have heard from me** in the presence of many witnesses entrust to faithful men who will be able to teach others also. (2 Tim 2.1–2)

Under the guidance of the specifically-commissioned apostles, the people of God in the New Testament lived and interacted and worked and worshiped together. They put into personal practice what they heard and saw in the apostles, much of which is recorded for us in the book of Acts and the various epistles. As a result, we can study historical examples of people who pleased God under the guidance of these Spirit-led ambassadors of Jesus.

What did they do?
How did they do it?
In what ways did they handle adversity and prosperity?
How were they corrected when they got off-track?
In what ways were they commended when they adhered to the pattern of sound words?

The principle behind Romans 15.4 holds true for us in this case. "Whatever was written in former days was written for our instruction, that through endurance and through the encouragement of the Scriptures we might have hope."

Undoubtedly, there are many examples preserved in the Bible that did not meet with God's approval. They are recorded—"warts and all"—for our learning and fearful avoidance.

A man named Ananias, with his wife Sapphira, sold a piece of property, and with his wife's knowledge, he kept back for himself some of the proceeds and brought only a part of it and laid it at the apostles' feet. (Acts 5.1–2)

But when Cephas came to Antioch, I opposed him to his face, because he stood condemned. (Gal 2.11)

It is actually reported that there is sexual immorality among you, and of a kind that is not tolerated even among pagans, for a man has his father's wife. And you are arrogant! Ought you not rather to mourn? Let him who has done this be removed from among you. (1 Cor 5.1–2)

The attitudes and actions that were complimented and encouraged by the original handpicked representatives of Jesus should be imitated by modern disciples of Christ. Those attitudes and actions that were condemned and prohibited by those Spirit-guided messengers should be warned against and avoided. These ancient examples of others serve as a vital connective path between God's will and modern discipleship.

Necessary Inferences

From the earliest of ages, we instinctively accumulate information based on instructions, examples and circumstances. Shaped by that information, we learn to make decisions and judgments. At times, we must make decisions and act in the absence of an express command or specific example. In such cases, we use our God-given powers of logical deduction. "Based on the data I have, what's the most natural conclusion to be drawn?"

The same holds for our approach to the Bible. Consider Acts 8.38.

And he commanded the chariot to stop, and they both went down into the water, Philip and the eunuch, and he baptized him.

Who baptized whom? We naturally infer from the language and context of Acts 8 that Philip baptized the eunuch rather than vice versa, even though the names are not specifically given.

Or consider the same principle intentionally employed by Paul to make a specific point.

> For the Scripture says, "Everyone who believes in him will not be put to shame." For there is no distinction between Jew and Greek; for the same Lord is Lord of all, bestowing his riches on all who call on him. For "everyone who calls on the name of the Lord will be saved."
>
> How then will they call on him in whom they have not believed? And how are they to believe in him of whom they have never heard? And how are they to hear without someone preaching? And how are they to preach unless they are sent? As it is written, "How beautiful are the feet of those who preach the good news!" (Rom 10.11–15)

Notice that Paul encourages his readers to remember the simple principle first established in Joel 2.32—everyone who calls on the name of the Lord will be saved. From there, he makes a series of necessary inferences in order to reinforce the importance of disciples preaching and supporting the preaching of the gospel.

> If people must call on the name of the Lord to be saved, we can necessarily infer that they *must* believe in him.
> If people are to believe in the Lord, we can necessarily infer that they *must* hear of him.
> If people are to hear of the Lord, someone *must* make a proclamation of him.
> "And how are they to preach unless they are sent?"

The writer of Hebrews relied heavily on necessary inferences to establish and repeatedly emphasize that the new covenant is "better" than the old. In fact, one of the great themes of Hebrews is that the old covenant taught by necessary inference that the new would be better.

In Mark 12.26–27, Jesus used the power of necessary inference to prove that those who have died continue to exist and will, in fact, be raised from the dead.

> And as for the dead being raised, have you not read in the book of Moses, in the passage about the bush, how God spoke to him, saying, 'I am the God of Abraham, and the God of Isaac, and the God of Jacob'? He is not God of the dead, but of the living. You are quite wrong.

God claimed to be the God of Abraham, Isaac and Jacob when he spoke to Moses from the bush.

At the point in history when God spoke to Moses from the bush, Abraham, Isaac and Jacob had been dead for many years.

We can necessarily infer from his statement that he is not God of the dead but of the living.

Therefore, the dead will be raised, and the Sadducees were quite wrong.

Of course, we must always honestly and consistently remind ourselves that not all inferences are necessary. Not all conclusions are inescapable. For example, some have used the accounts of Lydia, the Philippian jailer, and their households in Acts 16 as Scriptural authorization for the baptism of infants. Lydia was baptized, she "and her household" (16.15). The jailer was baptized at once, "he and all his family" (16.33). But to leap from those historical examples to Scriptural precedence for infant baptism is to infer that which is not necessary. There are many households without infants.

As we connect the dots between the Scriptures and God's authoritative will for our lives, we must make sure that our conclusions are resting on solid ground.

The Lord's Supper as a Case Study

No single passage of Scripture gives us every relevant detail regarding the observance of the Lord's Supper on the first day of every week. But as we familiarize ourselves with everything

God's word has to say on the subject, a well-developed pattern begins to emerge.

In 1 Corinthians 11.23–25, Paul delivers a **straightforward declaration of God-breathed truth**.

> For I received from the Lord what I also delivered to you, that the Lord Jesus on the night when he was betrayed took bread, and when he had given thanks, he broke it, and said, "This is my body which is for you. Do this in remembrance of me." In the same way also he took the cup, after supper, saying, "This cup is the new covenant in my blood. Do this, as often as you drink it, in remembrance of me."

In 1 Corinthians 11.26, we find an **overarching principle**.

> For as often as you eat this bread and drink the cup, you proclaim the Lord's death until he comes.

In 1 Corinthians 11.33–34, Paul conveys an **affirmative command**.

> So then, my brothers, when you come together to eat, wait for one another—if anyone is hungry, let him eat at home—so that when you come together it will not be for judgment.

1 Corinthians 11.20–22, carries the weight of **negative prohibition**.

> When you come together, it is not the Lord's supper that you eat. For in eating, each one goes ahead with his own meal. One goes hungry, another gets drunk. What! Do you not have houses to eat and drink in? Or do you despise the church of God and humiliate those who have nothing? What shall I say to you? Shall I commend you in this? No, I will not.

As to when this memorial was observed, Acts 20.7 provides an **approved example** from a historical account involving an inspired apostle.

> On the first day of the week, when we were gathered together to break bread, Paul talked with them, intending to depart on the next day, and he prolonged his speech until midnight.

From the days of Moses, God's people had been making a **necessary inference** as to the frequency of special observances. The Israelites understood that the command to "Remember the Sabbath day" (Exod 20.8) necessarily inferred a specific observance every seven days. If their observance was to be yearly, the month and the day were given (i.e. the Day of Atonement, Lev 23.27). If their observance was to be monthly, the day of the month was given (i.e. the blowing of silver trumpets, Num 10.10). If their observance was to be weekly, the day of the week was given (i.e. the seventh day, Exo 20.8–11). The New Testament proceeds according to the same logical pattern in passages like Acts 20.7 above and 1 Corinthians 16.1–2 below.

> Now concerning the collection for the saints: as I directed the churches of Galatia, so you also are to do. On the first day of every week, each of you is to put something aside and store it up, as he may prosper, so that there will be no collecting when I come.

Conclusion

We began this section of our study by asking some simple questions. How, practically speaking, does the Bible direct us? In real-life terms, how do we transition from reading God-breathed words on the printed pages of our Bibles to leading God-approved lives in our own modern context? Throughout the New Testament of Jesus Christ, we find six connective paths between the word of God and the human heart.

> Straightforward declarations of truth
> Overarching principles
> Affirmative commands
> Negative prohibitions
> Positive and negative examples
> Necessary inferences

> Be diligent to present yourself approved to God as a workman who does not need to be ashamed, accurately handling the word of truth. (2 Tim 2.15, NASB)

Questions for Growth and Discussion

1. List two or three examples of a **straightforward declaration of truth** in Scripture.

2. List two or three examples of an **overarching principle** in Scripture.

3. List two or three examples of **affirmative commands** in Scripture.

4. List two or three examples of **negative prohibitions** in Scripture.

5. List two or three examples of **positive examples** in Scripture.

6. List two or three examples of **negative examples** in Scripture.

7. List two or three examples where **inference is necessary** in Scripture.

8. Take the time to read Luke's historical account of the controversy over circumcision in Acts 15. Volatile questions swirled around the life of the early church as to whether Gentile Christians had to be circumcised in order to be pleasing to God (15.5). Using the text of Acts 15, can you find an instance where each of the six connective paths mentioned in this study were employed to discover and clarify God's will?

   * A straightforward declaration of truth
   * An overarching principle
   * Affirmative commands
   * Negative prohibitions
   * An approved example
   * A necessary inference

eight

Applying Heavenly Authority to Everyday Life

As human beings, we understand and apply authoritative instructions using everyday common sense. We learn to do so from a very early age. We may not use distinctive labels or philosophical definitions to describe what we're doing, but we comprehend and follow the fundamental principles of authority and compliance in thousands upon thousands of actions and reactions over a lifetime of interaction.

For example, a father knocks on the bedroom door of his teenage son and communicates clear instructions to him. "Take this $25 and go to Pizza Hut on Main Street. I just called in an order for a sausage pizza, an order of breadsticks, and a Diet Coke. Go straight there, and come straight back home. We'll have the table set when you get back." That teenager is now the recipient of very **specific** instructions that carry the authoritative weight of his father. These instructions, by their very nature, logically rule out millions of other variables.

Can the teenage son take his father's $25, pick up his girlfriend, and head for the movie theater? No! Why not? His father specifically told him to go to Pizza Hut and spend the money there. Even though his father did not methodically list every possible place his son should *not* go, the teenager naturally understands something, doesn't he? To take that $25 and spend it anywhere other than Pizza Hut will be to disobey his father at home. His father's **specific** mention of Pizza Hut on Main Street **logically rules out** every other pizza place, every other restaurant, every other venue, and even every other Pizza Hut other than the Pizza Hut on Main Street.

The same principle applies to the sausage pizza, the order of breadsticks, and the Diet Coke. If the teenager comes home with a pepperoni pizza, an order of hot wings, and a Mountain Dew, he will have failed to follow his father's instructions. Why? Even though the teenager went to Pizza Hut, his father **specifically** ordered a sausage pizza, breadsticks, and a Diet Coke. The specific nature of his communication **logically rules out** every other kind of pizza, every other side item, and every other beverage.

"Go straight there, and come straight back home" were his father's final **specific** instructions. Even *if* the teenager goes to Pizza Hut, to go anywhere other than Pizza Hut will be to blatantly disregard his father's instructions. Why? All other stops are **logically ruled out** by the specific instructions of his authoritative father.

As a human being, the teenage son has freedom of will. He has received specific instructions from his father. The way he acts from the point of instruction forward depends entirely on the level of respect he has for his father.

On the other hand, suppose the same father knocks on the bedroom door of the same teenage son with similar but more **general** instructions. "Your mom is in the mood for pizza. How about taking this $25 and picking one up for all of us? And while you're at it, grab some dessert and a soft drink or two." That teenager has received some very **generic** instructions that carry the authoritative weight of his father. He is still expected to go and pick up some pizza with the money provided, but the nature of his father's instructions logically carry a certain amount of freedom to choose how those instructions will be carried out.

Pepperoni? Sausage? Supreme? Hawaiian? Cheese? Any one of these—including a number of other options—are available to the teenager, as long as he comes home with a pizza.

Ice cream? Cookies? Cake? Brownies? Candy? Any of these—

including a number of other options—are available to the teenager, as long as he comes home with some type of dessert. His father has no logical right to be upset with his son if the teenager comes home with vanilla ice cream instead of Milky Way candy bars. Why not? He gave his son **generic** instructions. "Grab some dessert." The category of dessert was assigned, but **anything within that category** is a fulfillment of the father's instructions.

Where should he buy the dessert? Pizza Hut? Dairy Queen? A grocery store? A gas station? Any of these—including a number of other options—are available to the teenager, as long as he comes home with dessert. The source of the dessert was not limited by specific instructions from his father.

Coke? Pepsi? Dr. Pepper? Mountain Dew? Sprite? Any of these—including a number of other options—are available to the teenager, as long as he comes home with a 2-liter … or two. Neither the type (plastic bottles, cans, etc.) nor the size (2-liter, 16 oz., etc.) nor a specific number of containers were specified. "A soft drink or two" were the **general** instructions provided by his father.

The difference between **specific** and **generic** instructions from an authority figure isn't hard to discern, is it? **Specific instructions specify.** By their very nature, they exclude and rule out every other option.

Your Last Will and Testament specifies *who* is to receive *what* in your inheritance. It doesn't list everyone who is excluded from your inheritance.

The deed to your property specifies the *owner* of the property. It doesn't list everyone without a claim to your property.

The prescription you got from your doctor specifies the medication you *can* receive from your pharmacist. It doesn't list every single medication that's off-limits to you in your present condition.

Your airline ticket specifies *who* can board an airplane and *where* that flight is headed. It doesn't list everyone without a right to board, nor does it list every city that isn't included in your destination.

On the other hand, **generic instructions generalize.** By their very nature, they include any number of options within a specific group, category, or class.

Elementary teachers provide supply lists at the start of a school year. "Five folders" on the list provides general instruction with many options. The brand, color, and texture of the folders are up to the student, as long as he or she brings five folders to school.

The college professor who assigns a biography term-paper to his students has provided generic instructions. Each student can select from millions of options, as long he or she writes a term-paper that is biographical in nature.

The boss who sends an intern out of the office to buy a box of 8.5" x 11" paper has provided general instructions. The intern has a choice as to where he or she purchases the paper, as long as the paper is purchased.

The father who tells his son to fill up the gas tank of the car before bringing it back home after the Friday night date has provided general instructions. The gas station used by the son is up to the son, as long as the gas tank is full when he pulls the car into the driveway.

Specific Authority in the Bible

It is God who created human beings with the ability to understand and apply authoritative instructions using everyday common sense. He equipped us to comprehend and follow the fundamental principles of authority in thousands upon thousands of actions and reactions in everyday life. And he used the same principles in his authoritative written communication to mankind.

As created image-bearers, our heavenly Father has blessed us with freedom of will. He has given us some very specific instructions. The way we conduct ourselves during our time on the earth will depend, in large part, on the level of respect we have for our Father.

Take your time with the following chart. It illustrates, using Old and New Testament examples, the premise behind and the power of specific commands and examples. When God gave precise instructions or preserved examples that were approved under the oversight of inspired representatives, those commands and examples logically excluded variations in thought and behavior. We can learn how to apply heavenly authority to everyday life by learning from the examples of those who came before us.

These Specific COMMANDS or EXAMPLES	Logically Exclude These VARIATIONS
Noah (Gen 6.14) Make yourself an ark	A house, wall, tower, well, altar
Of gopher wood	Oak, poplar, cedar, pine, olive wood
Abraham (Gen 22.2) Offer Isaac as a burnt offering	Sarah, Ishmael, Hagar, a servant, himself, a lamb or any other animal
Passover (Exod 12) Sacrifice a lamb	A bull, a heifer, a bird, a pig, a person
Without blemish	Any sort of blemish
One year old	Any age younger or older than one year old
Male	Female
On the 14th day of the first month	Every other day of the year

Purification (Num 19.1–2) A red heifer	Any other animal or heifer of another color
Without defect	Any defect
On which a yoke has never come	Any red heifer who had borne a yoke
Proclaim (Mark 16.15–16) The gospel	Human traditions, philosophies, opinions, speculations, politics
To the whole creation	To only a certain gender, race or class
Belief and baptism	A "good moral life," the Sinner's Prayer, the Ten Commandments, belief alone
Baptism A burial (Rom 6.4)	Sprinkling, pouring
In water (Acts 8.36; 10.47)	Into Moses, of the Holy Spirit, of fire
For the forgiveness of sins (Acts 2.38)	To be added to a church, as an outward sign of an inward grace
Assemblies of Christians for Worship The Lord's Supper (1 Cor 11.25) Prayer (Acts 2.42) Singing (Eph 5.19) Teaching (Acts 20.7) Collection for the saints (1 Cor 16.1–2)	Animal sacrifices, burning of incense, counting of beads, adoration of images, secular entertainment, exalting of people, politics, social work, sports and recreation

The Lord's Supper	
On the first day of the week (Acts 20.7)	Any other day of the week
Bread and fruit of the vine (Matt 26.26–29)	Roasted lamb, bitter herbs, eggs, or any other food or beverage
The Church's Raising of Funds (2 Cor 9.6–7) Voluntary giving of Christians	Suppers, raffles, carnivals, car washes, business operations, real estate, begging from visitors

As we make decisions from within a secular and religious culture plagued with spiritual ADD (Authority Deficit Disorder), let's be careful to reverently and consistently apply heavenly authority to our everyday lives.

Questions for Growth and Discussion

1. Can you think of a way that you recently understood and applied authoritative instructions using everyday common sense?

2. We expect children, from a very early age, to grow in their ability to comprehend and comply with basic instructions. Why?

3. Specific instructions from an authoritative figure naturally exclude and rule out other options and variables. Why?

4. What role does respect play in the following of specific instructions from an authoritative figure?

5. Generic instructions from an authoritative figure naturally include any number of options within a specific group, category, or class. Why?

6. Four examples were offered to illustrate how specific instructions specify. Can you think of some additional examples to further illustrate the point?

7. Four examples were offered to illustrate how generic instructions generalize. Can you think of some additional examples to further illustrate the point?

8. What role does the freedom of human will play in applying heavenly authority to everyday life?

9. A number of commands or documented examples were offered from the Old Testament to illustrate the nature of specific instruction. Can you think of other Old Testament examples to illustrate the point?

10. A number of commands or documented examples were offered from the New Testament to illustrate the nature of specific instruction. Can you think of other New Testament examples to illustrate the point?

nine

On the Making of Expedient Judgments

An "expedient" is an appropriate, profitable, advantageous way to accomplish something. Expedients are helpful means to necessary ends. The word *expedient* is used seven times in the King James Version of the Scriptures.

> Nor consider that it is **expedient** for us, that one man should die for the people, and that the whole nation perish not. (John 11.50)

> Nevertheless I tell you the truth; it is **expedient** for you that I go away: for if I go not away, the Comforter will not come unto you; but if I depart, I will send him unto you. (John 16.7)

> Now Caiaphas was he, which gave counsel to the Jews, that it was **expedient** that one man should die for the people. (John 18.14)

> All things are lawful unto me, but all things are not **expedient**: all things are lawful for me, but I will not be brought under the power of any. (1 Cor 6.12)

> All things are lawful for me, but all things are not **expedient**: all things are lawful for me, but all things edify not. (1 Cor 10.23)

> And herein I give my advice: for this is **expedient** for you, who have begun before, not only to do, but also to be forward a year ago. (2 Cor 8.10)

It is not **expedient** for me doubtless to glory. I will come to visions and revelations of the Lord. (2 Cor 12.1)

The English Standard Version translates *sumphero* (Greek) in the passages listed above as **"better"** (John 11.50), **"to your advantage"** (John 16.7), **"expedient"** (John 18.14), **"helpful"** (1 Cor 6.12; 10.23), **"benefits"** (2 Cor 8.10), and **"to be gained"** (2 Cor 12.1). As a noun, *sumpheros* (Greek) is also used by Paul in 1 Corinthians, and noting the context deepens our understanding of the principle behind the word.

> I want you to be free from anxieties. The unmarried man is anxious about the things of the Lord, how to please the Lord. But the married man is anxious about worldly things, how to please his wife, and his interests are divided. And the unmarried or betrothed woman is anxious about the things of the Lord, how to be holy in body and spirit. But the married woman is anxious about worldly things, how to please her husband. I say this for your own **benefit**, not to lay any restraint upon you, but to promote good order and to secure your undivided devotion to the Lord. (1 Cor 7.32–35)

> So, whether you eat or drink, or whatever you do, do all to the glory of God. Give no offense to Jews or to Greeks or to the church of God, just as I try to please everyone in everything I do, not seeking my own **advantage**, but that of many, that they may be saved (1 Cor 10.31–33).

Based on our study up to this point, we know that God hasn't given mankind a blank check labeled "EXPEDIENT." If in all circumstances he allowed us to determine for ourselves what is right and wrong within the boundaries of our own view of what is "better," "beneficial" or "advantageous," we would basically become a law unto ourselves and do whatever was right in our own eyes.

And yet, God *has* allowed us to choose for ourselves how a number of generic commands will be carried out and general examples will be modeled in our own modern context. Some aspects of discipleship can be accurately and faithfully described and fulfilled as matters of human judgment. In such cases, we have liberty to judge what would be most appropriate, profitable and advantageous in a given situation. We have freedom to ask, "What would be the most helpful and beneficial means of reaching this necessary end?"

Constructive Questions to Ask in the Making of Expedient Judgments

Is it lawful? "'All things are lawful,' but not all things are helpful" (1 Cor 10.23). Some of the early Christians in Corinth were arguing that all things were lawful for the Christian. There was great confusion and argument over how to view meat that had been sacrificed to a pagan idol. Paul provides practical instruction in the larger context of 1 Corinthians 10, but establishes that things must first and foremost be "lawful." Before we consider whether a thing is expedient, we must honestly ask, "Is it lawful?" If it's not lawful, it can't be expedient.

Has God been specific? If something has been specified, there is no room for expedients.

Is it helpful? In 1 Corinthians 10, the Spirit encourages us to recognize that even lawful things may not be helpful in a specific situation. Some press their opinion or insist on their "pet project" in the name of expediency even if it causes division among God's people. Such attitudes and actions destroy rather than edify and build up (1 Cor 14.26).

Will this cause my brother or sister to stumble? In 1 Corinthians 10.32, Paul qualifies his instructions about expediencies by saying, "Give no offense to Jews or to Greeks or to the church of God." In 1 Corinthians 8.7–13 he encourages careful recognition that "not all possess" mature knowledge and that the mature must act accordingly.

> And so by your knowledge this weak person is destroyed, the brother for whom Christ died. Thus, sinning against your brothers and wounding their conscience when it is weak, you sin against Christ. Therefore, if food makes my brother stumble, I will never eat meat, lest I make my brother stumble. (1 Cor 8.11–13)

These General COMMANDS or EXAMPLES	Logically Encourage the Question of EXPEDIENCY
Noah (Gen 6.14) Make yourself an ark	The tools Noah was to use were not specified; Noah could use whatever was available, as long as it did not violate other clear communication from God
The Great Commission (Matt 28.19–20) Go	Jesus did not specify how his disciples were to go; walking, riding, sailing, flying, even the Internet can faciliate the going
Baptizing	Jesus did not specify the physical location of baptism; rivers, lakes, bathtubs, pools, and baptistries
Teaching	Teaching can be accomplished in so many ways today: around kitchen tables, in classrooms, with printed materials, audio-visual resources, radio, the Internet, etc.
Assembling with the Saints Not neglecting to meet together (Heb 10.25)	A very practical question every group of disciples faces is, "Where?" Outdoors? In a private house? A rented hall? In a meeting house of their own?

The Lord's Supper On the first day of the week (Acts 20.7)	But at what time on the first day of the week?
Addressing one another in song (Eph 5.19; Col 3.16)	Will we sing from memory? Will we use song books? Will we project the songs on a screen? Will we have a leader who selects the songs and gets us started?

Questions for Growth and Discussion

1. In your own words, what does the word "expedient" mean?

2. What sort of expedient things have you used even this very day?

3. Why was it "expedient" that Jesus should "go away" (John 16.7)?

4. In 1 Corinthians 6.12 and 10.23, the apostle Paul emphasized that "all things are not expedient." Is that still true? And how can we know?

5. In your own words, summarize Paul's communication in 1 Corinthians 7.32–35.

6. Why is the attitude manifested in 1 Corinthians 10.31–33 still worthy of imitation?

7. "Is it lawful?" Why must we always be willing to start with and return to that question?

8. "Will this cause my brother or sister to stumble?" Why must I be willing to honestly ask and seriously consider that question?

9. Can you think of some additional Old Testament examples to illustrate the principle that general commands or examples logically encourage the question of expediency?

10. Can you think of some additional New Testament examples to illustrate the principle that general commands or examples logically encourage the question of expediency?

ten

Walking in the Footsteps of Biblical Examples

As we wind down the application portion of our study, one more issue ought to be addressed. When it comes to the examples we find in the New Testament, for what should we be looking? Which details within those examples, if any, should we treat as timeless and applicable to our own context? How can we discern which elements of any given Biblical account are simply incidental—necessary for understanding the narrative, but not intended to be followed as a model—and which ones have been preserved by God so that we might follow in the same footsteps?

From time to time, it's helpful to rigorously analyze the detailed historical accounts of the Bible with those sorts of questions in mind. Careful, honest analysis can protect us from carelessly concluding that nothing but dry history is contained in the examples of the earliest disciples. And we may even find ourselves equipped to recognize some overlooked intricacies within those powerful models of the past.

A Case Study

Consider Luke's historical account in Acts 20.1–8.

After the uproar ceased, Paul sent for the disciples, and after encouraging them, he said farewell and departed for Macedonia. When he had gone through those regions and had given them much encouragement, he came to Greece. There he spent three months, and when a plot was made against him by the

Jews as he was about to set sail for Syria, he decided to return through Macedonia. Sopater the Berean, son of Pyrrhus, accompanied him; and of the Thessalonians, Aristarchus and Secundus; and Gaius of Derbe, and Timothy; and the Asians, Tychicus and Trophimus. These went on ahead and were waiting for us at Troas, but we sailed away from Philippi after the days of Unleavened Bread, and in five days we came to them at Troas, where we stayed for seven days.

On the first day of the week, when we were gathered together to break bread, Paul talked with them, intending to depart the next day, and he prolonged his speech until midnight. There were many lamps in the upper room where we were gathered.

Luke has preserved quite a few details for us in the last two sentences of that account alone.

It was the first day of the week.
The disciples were gathered together.
They had gathered together to break bread.
Paul addressed the disciples who were gathered together.
He intended to depart the next day.
He prolonged his speech until midnight.
The disciples were gathered in an upper room.
There were many lamps in the upper room.

Take the time to carefully think about those details. How should we, as modern disciples of Christ, treat them? Which of those details, if any, should be applied today? Should they *all* be applied? If not, which ones should be applied, and how can we know? Here they are again. Which of those details continue to carry modern significance and which of them are simply incidental—necessary for an understanding of the historical narrative?

It was the first day of the week.
The disciples were gathered together.
They had gathered together to break bread.
Paul addressed the disciples who were gathered.
He intended to depart the next day.

He prolonged his speech until midnight.

The disciples were gathered in an upper room.

There were many lamps in the upper room.

What About the Place?

Most of us would immediately attach spiritual significance to the time of the disciples' gathering but not the place. But why does the time have enduring significance while the place is treated as incidental? We suppose the fact that these disciples met on the first day of the week is instructive. Is that a reasonable supposition? And if so, why isn't the fact that they met in an upper room also instructive? After all, the only other occasion in Scripture that a place is connected with the Lord's Supper, an upper room was involved.

> And on the first day of Unleavened Bread, when they sacrificed the Passover lamb, his disciples said to him, "Where will you have us go and prepare for you to eat the Passover?" And he sent two of his disciples and said to them, "Go into the city, and a man carrying a jar of water will meet you. Follow him, and wherever he enters, say to the master of the house, 'The Teacher says, Where is my guest room, where I may eat the Passover with my disciples?' And he will show you a large upper room furnished and ready; there prepare for us." (Mark 14.12–15)

It was in this upper room, "as they were eating," that Jesus took bread, and after blessing it, broke it and gave it to his disciples, and said, "Take; this is my body." And he took a cup, and when he had given thanks he gave it to them, and they all drank of it. And he said to them, "This is my blood of the covenant, which is poured out for many. Truly, I say to you, I will not drink again of the fruit of the vine until that day when I drink it new in the kingdom of God" (Mark 14.22–25). Do these two references to an upper room constitute a pattern? Is the upper room detail of the Acts 20 example preserved that we might follow suit?

Several years ago, Jeff Smelser published an excellent article wherein he suggested two important questions that should be asked in view of Biblical examples. These questions don't necessarily yield enlightenment in every instance where we seek to determine what is intended by Scripture, but they do illustrate how we can reasonably ascertain the purpose of the inclusion of certain details or facts within the Biblical narrative. Applying the questions to the Acts 20 example:

1. Do the requirements of the narrative provide sufficient reason for the mention of the place?

2. Is there spiritual significance attached to the place?

In answer to the second question, there is no obvious spiritual significance attached to the upper room. On the other hand, if we read further in Acts 20, we can see narrative-related reasons for the mention of an upper room.

> And a young man named Eutychus, sitting at the window, sank into a deep sleep as Paul talked still longer. And being overcome by sleep, he fell down from the third story and was taken up dead. But Paul went down and bent over him, and taking him in his arms, said, "Do not be alarmed, for his life is in him." And when Paul had gone up and had broken bread and eaten, he conversed with them a long while, until daybreak, and so departed. And they took the youth away alive, and were not a little comforted. (Acts 20.9–12)

In Acts 20, the fact that the disciples were gathered in an upper room is significant in relation to Eutychus' fall and the miracle subsequently performed. In Mark 14.12–15, Jesus' mentioning of the specific details of the room is comparable with his mentioning that the man they would find in the city would be carrying a jar of water. In other words, the events would unfold exactly as Jesus foretold in every detail, thus calling attention to the hand of God in all that was transpiring.

The same point can be illustrated by Samuel's meticulously detailed instructions to Saul in 1 Samuel 10.1–7.

Then Samuel took a flask of oil and poured it on [Saul's] head and kissed him and said, "Has not the Lord anointed you to be prince over his people Israel? And you shall reign over the people of the Lord and you will save them from the hand of their surrounding enemies. And this shall be the sign to you that the Lord has anointed you to be prince over his heritage. When you depart from me today, you will meet two men by Rachel's tomb in the territory of Benjamin at Zelzah, and they will say to you, 'The donkeys that you went to seek are found, and now your father has ceased to care about the donkeys and is anxious about you, saying, "What shall I do about my son?"' Then you shall go on from there farther and come to the oak of Tabor. Three men going up to God at Bethel will meet you there, one carrying three young goats, another carrying three loaves of bread, and another carrying a skin of wine. And they will greet you and give you two loaves of bread, which you shall accept from their hand. After that you shall come to Gibeath-elohim, where there is a garrison of the Philistines. And there, as soon as you come to the city, you will meet a group of prophets coming down from the high place with harp, tambourine, flute, and lyre before them, prophesying. Then the Spirit of the Lord will rush upon you, and you will prophesy with them and be turned into another man. Now when these signs meet you, do what your hand finds to do, for God is with you.

In this instance, it wasn't the three loaves of bread and the skin of wine themselves that were significant, nor the harp, tambourine, flute or lyre. Rather, it was significant that the events unfolded just as Samuel had said they would.

So also, in Mark 14.15, it wasn't the place itself that was significant. Jesus, in response to the Samaritan woman's queries about worshiping on "this mountain" or "that mountain" had already established that "God is spirit, and those who worship him must worship in spirit and truth," regardless of the physical location (John 4.19–24). Of primary significance in Mark 14 is that the events unfolded just as Jesus had said they would (Mark 14.16), including the fact that the two disciples were led to an upper room.

It's not surprising that both the Passover supper on the eve of Jesus' crucifixion and the gathering of the Troas disciples to break bread took place in upper rooms. There is ample historical and cultural evidence that the upper rooms of a house were the most desirable, especially in the warmer months, for such an occasion and that such rooms were regularly reserved for guests.

So we have every reason to suppose the elevation of the room was what would be expected by convention and no reason to suppose the elevation had any spiritual significance. On both occasions, we have every reason to suppose the elevation was mentioned for our comprehension of the narrative and no reason to suppose the elevation of the room was mentioned as precedent for us.

What About the Day?

On the other hand, do the requirements of the narrative provide sufficient reason for the mention of the day? Is there spiritual significance attached to the day?

Taking the first question first, the narrative in Acts 20 hardly requires mention of the day of the week in verse 7. Luke is telling us about Paul's third journey. Throughout the book of Acts, as Luke relates the events of Paul's various journeys, he carefully indicates where Paul went, sometimes explaining in detail the route followed, certainly making clear the chronology. A number of significant events are described. On several occasions, Luke does note that it was the Sabbath day, but the significance of the day was that it was the occasion Paul could expect to find Jews assembled at the synagogue (Acts 13.14, 42–44; 16.13; 18.4). Aside from those references to the Sabbath day, not once in the book of Acts does Luke ever feel the need to indicate on which day of the week something occurred other than in Acts 20.7. And in that passage, knowledge of the day of the week in no way helps us to understand anything else in the passage, unless it be the nature of the meal the disciples came together to eat. And then, knowledge of the day of the week only helps in our understanding if indeed it can be supposed that it has spiritual significance.

Therefore, let us consider the second question: Is there spiritual significance attached to the day?

Note, first of all, Jesus was raised from the dead on the first day of the week, and this fact is mentioned in Matthew, Mark, Luke, and John.

> Now after the Sabbath, toward the dawn of **the first day of the week**, Mary Magdalene and the other Mary went to see the tomb. (Matt 28.1)

> When the Sabbath was past, Mary Magdalene and Mary the mother of James and Salome bought spices, so that they might go and anoint him. And very early on **the first day of the week**, when the sun had risen, they went to the tomb. (Mark 16.1–2)

> But on **the first day of the week**, at early dawn, they went to the tomb, taking the spices they had prepared. (Luke 24.1)

> Now on **the first day of the week** Mary Magdalene came to the tomb early, while it was still dark, and saw that the stone had been taken away from the tomb. (John 20.1)

Jesus' first appearance to the twelve (minus Judas and Thomas, but with the addition of Cleopas and his companion) was on "the very day" of his resurrection, the first day of the week (Luke 24.13–43; John 20.19–25). It was on the next first day of the week that Jesus again appeared to them, this time with Thomas present (John 20.26). Then, six weeks later, the evidence suggests it was on the first day of the week that the gospel was publicly proclaimed for the first time after Jesus' resurrection. We conclude this primarily because the day of Pentecost was to be observed on the day after the seventh Sabbath following Passover (Lev 23.15–16).

The first day of the week was the Lord's day of victory over death, a victory which was of preeminent importance. By that victory, he was declared to be the Son of God (Rom 1.4). By that victory, God has given assurance that he will judge the world in righteousness by Jesus (Acts 17.31). By that victory, Jesus destroyed the one who has the power of death, that is, the devil (Heb 2.14). Therefore, when John referred to a particular day in which he was "in the Spirit" as "the Lord's day" (Rev 1.10), it is only reasonable to understand he was speaking of the first day of the week.

Moreover, we know the church at Corinth, and apparently also the churches of Galatia, regularly assembled on the first day of the week (1 Cor 16.1–2), the Lord's day. And finally, we know that supper in which the saints commemorated the Lord's death was known as the "Lord's Supper" (1 Cor 11.20), a term which quite naturally connects it with the "Lord's day," which, as noted above, must have been the first day of the week.

When we come to Acts 20.7 and see Luke noting it was on the first day of the week that the disciples came together to break bread, we readily conclude the breaking of the bread was the observance of the Lord's Supper. But we come to that conclusion because we have first of all discerned the significance of the first day of the week. That was a day that had great spiritual significance.

Having established the spiritual significance of the day, and having found no reason for the mention of the day apart from its spiritual significance, we can be confident that Luke's mentioning of the first day of the week in Acts 20 is profoundly instructive. It is not merely a random detail included to enable our comprehension of the narrative. It is something to which God draws our attention throughout the New Testament that we might notice and follow with understanding and reverence.

Conclusion

Much of what has been said in this chapter is intuitive. We don't always have to methodically analyze a passage of Scripture to recognize what the intended point is. Our habits of human communication enable us to intuitively comprehend the point.

But, from time to time, it is helpful to rigorously analyze why one example is instructive while another is not. These types of exercises will protect us from concluding that we can't expect to find any instruction in the examples of the Bible. And they may even equip us to recognize some overlooked elements of God's providentially-preserved revelation to mankind.

Questions for Growth and Discussion

1. Acts 20.7 tells us the disciples were gathered together "to break bread." What does Luke intend for us to understand by that reference?

2. Luke told us in Acts 2.42 that the earliest Christians "devoted themselves to the apostles' teaching and the fellowship, to the breaking of bread and the prayers." In your own words, to what were these disciples devoted?

3. Just a few verses later, Luke tells us that the disciples were "breaking bread in their homes" (Acts 2.46). Is this reference to "breaking bread" different from the reference in Acts 2.42? If so, in what way?

4. What should we make of Luke's mentioning in Acts 20.7 of Paul prolonging his speech until midnight?

5. And what about the presence of "many lamps" in the upper room (Acts 20.8)? Do the requirements of the narrative provide sufficient reason for the mention of the lamps? Should any spiritual significance be attached to the lamps?

6. Observances of the Passover would include more than unleavened bread and fruit of the vine. If roasted lamb and bitter herbs were elements of Jesus' last meal with the disciples, why are they not also a part of the Lord's Supper?

7. Samuel's meticulously detailed instructions to Saul in 1 Samuel 10.1–7 were offered as an example of calling attention to God's handiwork before an event actually occurred. Can you think of other Old or New Testament examples that establish the same point?

8. Take the time to read John 4.19–24. What should we take away from Jesus' answer to the Samaritan woman's query?

9. Is there ongoing spiritual significance attached to the first

day of the week for modern disciples of Jesus? If so, why? If not, why not?

10. John 13 documents Jesus washing the feet of his disciples on the evening of the Passover. What about that example? How should it be handled? Should it be modeled and mimicked by modern disciples?

eleven

When God Hasn't Said Anything About It

Having focused extensively in previous lessons on the nature of God's specific and generic instructions, we turn our attention more fully to the other end of the spectrum. What about those innumerable instances when God *hasn't* said anything? How should we treat the silence of God? Is it permissive or prohibitive? When God hasn't specifically addressed something in either positive or negative terms, may we faithfully interpret his silence as license to proceed in whatever direction we choose?

Granted, we don't read anything in God's revelation to mankind about the yearly observance of Easter, but what's the big deal if we're remembering Jesus? The use of guitars, keyboards and drums in our corporate gatherings of worship can't be specifically authorized using the New Testament, but what's wrong with using them if our praise is enthusiastically directed toward God? May we build whatever we would like to build, fund whatever we would like to fund, solicit in whatever way we would like to solicit, as long as some justifiable good comes as a result of our efforts?

As human beings, we can formulate an endless amount of "good reasons." Given enough time and wiggle room, we can justify nearly anything. We can appeal to emotions and reason from past experiences and motivate with inspiring rhetoric, but *we* are not the ultimate standard of authority. The bedrock principles delivered in Isaiah 55.6–11 continue to resonate throughout the created order:

Seek the LORD while he may be found;
  call upon him while he is near;
let the wicked forsake his way,
  and the unrighteous man his thoughts;
let him return to the LORD, that he may have compassion on him,
  and to our God, for he will abundantly pardon.
For my thoughts are not your thoughts,
  neither are your ways my ways, declares the LORD.
For as the heavens are higher than the earth,
  so are my ways higher than your ways
  and my thoughts than your thoughts.

For as the rain and the snow come down from heaven
  and do not return there but water the earth,
making it bring forth and sprout,
  giving seed to the sower and bread to the eater,
so shall my word be that goes out from my mouth;
  it shall not return to me empty,
but it shall accomplish that which I purpose,
  and shall succeed in the thing for which I sent it.

Words from the mouth of the Creator have been delivered to and preserved for his creation. There is divine purpose behind his revealed thoughts and demonstrated ways. He has already told us his ways and thoughts are inherently distinct from our ways and thoughts. They are higher and holier. His purposes will be accomplished; his will shall succeed. Our responsibility, as repeatedly referenced in this study, is simple and straightforward.

Look carefully then how you walk, not as unwise but as wise, making the best use of the time, because the days are evil. Therefore do not be foolish, but understand what the will of the Lord is. (Eph 5.15–17)

In the end, therefore, the question is infinitely bigger than "Why can't we?" or "What's the big deal?" Despite our opinions, justifications, and rationalizations, the only thing that truly matters in the final analysis is this: how does God treat his silence in the Scriptures? Is it prohibitive or permissive?

The Sounds of Silence in the Old Testament

In Exodus 14, the people of Israel stood on the brink of freedom. Having been delivered from Egyptian bondage, they had been led by Moses to the shores of the Red Sea. What they didn't realize was that Pharaoh had changed his mind about allowing them to be free.

> The Egyptians pursued them, all Pharaoh's horses and chariots and his horsemen and his army, and overtook them encamped at the sea, by Pi-hahiroth, in front of Baal-zephon.
>
> When Pharaoh drew near, the people of Israel lifted up their eyes, and behold, the Egyptians were marching after them, and they feared greatly. And the people of Israel cried out to the Lord. They said to Moses, "Is it because there are no graves in Egypt that you have taken us away to die in the wilderness? What have you done to us in bringing us out of Egypt? Is not this what we said to you in Egypt: 'Leave us alone that we may serve the Egyptians'? For it would have been better for us to serve the Egyptians than to die in the wilderness." And Moses said to the people, "Fear not, stand firm, and see the salvation of the Lord, which he will work for you today. For the Egyptians whom you see today, you shall never see again. The Lord will fight for you, and you have only to be silent." (Exod 14.9–14)

What did God want them to do? Wait. Wait for further instruction. Fear not, stand firm, and wait for the salvation of the Lord. How long should they wait? Until they received the command to move. Even if Pharaoh was in sight? Even if Pharaoh was in sight. What if the command to move didn't come? Fear not. Stand firm. Wait. God will deliver you. He knows what he's doing.

> The Lord said to Moses, "Why do you cry to me? Tell the people of Israel to go forward. Lift up your staff, and stretch out your hand over the sea and divide it, that the people of Israel may go through the sea on dry ground. And I will harden the hearts of the Egyptians so that they shall go in after them, and

I will get glory over Pharaoh and all his host, his chariots, and his horsemen. And the Egyptians shall know that I am the Lord, when I have gotten glory over Pharaoh, his chariots, and his horsemen." (Exod 14.15–18)

When God's people wait for God's instructions so that they might fulfill God's purposes, God gets the glory.

In Numbers 9, the children of Israel had made their way to Mount Sinai. It had been a year since they had observed the first Passover in Egypt.

And the Lord spoke to Moses in the wilderness of Sinai, in the first month of the second year after they had come out of the land of Egypt, saying, "Let the people of Israel keep the Passover at its appointed time. On the fourteenth day of this month, at twilight, you shall keep it at its appointed time; according to all its statutes and all its rules you shall keep it." So Moses told the people of Israel that they should keep the Passover. And they kept the Passover in the first month, on the fourteenth day of the month, at twilight, in the wilderness of Sinai; according to all that the Lord commanded Moses, so the people of Israel did. And there were certain men who were unclean through touching a dead body, so that they could not keep the Passover on that day, and they came before Moses and Aaron on that day. And those men said to him, "We are unclean through touching a dead body. Why are we kept from bringing the Lord's offering at its appointed time among the people of Israel?" And Moses said to them, "Wait, that I may hear what the Lord will command concerning you." (Num 9.1–8)

"Why can't we?" is not a novel religious question. For centuries, men and women have faced choices of practical conduct in light of God's revelation. "Knowing what I know, what will I do?" "Having heard what I've heard, how should I proceed?" "If God hasn't addressed it, why can't I?"

These "certain men," had a choice to make. In Numbers 5.1–4, the Lord had already commanded the people of Israel to put out of the camp everyone who was unclean through contact with the dead. But it was Passover! A national celebration! And yes, this is what the LORD had specifically said, but did it really apply in this instance? Didn't this extraordinary situation overshadow what God had dictated in the law? "Why can't we?" was the question put to Moses.

Moses' response? Wait. God's silence on this specific nuance of law and conduct is significant. We shouldn't presume. We shouldn't rationalize. We should wait and seek clarification from the LORD before we act. And in Numbers 9.9–14, God provided his answer, granting special permission for the men's observance one month later. But what would have happened if these men had interpreted God's silence as license to act? Multiple Old Testament examples suggest the consequences could have been disastrous.

In Deuteronomy 28–30, Moses delivered some of his final instructions and warnings to the people of Israel. In Deuteronomy 28.1–14, he established the blessings that would naturally come as a result of faithful obedience to the voice of the LORD. In Deuteronomy 28.15–68, he extensively elaborated on the curses that would consume the people if they did not obey. The principles behind his communication are simple and straightforward—if God said do it, do it! If God said don't do it, don't do it! Whether God had communicated something specifically or generically, the people were to respect his revelation. And as for the things he hadn't said?

> The secret things belong to the LORD our God, but the things that are revealed belong to us and to our children forever, that we may do all the words of this law. (Deut 29.29)

If God revealed it, it belongs to us, and our responsibility is to act. If God didn't reveal it, the secret things belong to the LORD, and his silence is not a license for action.

> Everything that I command you, you shall be careful to do. You shall not add to it or take from it. (Deut 12.32)

One of the holy vessels of the tabernacle system was the ark of the covenant. The LORD had "set apart the tribe of Levi to carry the ark of the covenant of the LORD to stand before the LORD to minister to him" (Deut 10.8). The LORD didn't say, "men from the tribes of Reuben, Simeon, Judah and Dan shall not carry the ark of the covenant." But then again, a "thou shalt not" was unnecessary. By specifying the tribe of Levi as authorized, all other tribes of Israel were logically excluded.

Was God's silence concerning the rights of the tribes of Naphtali, Gad and Asher to carry the ark prohibitive? Listen to the logic of David, a man after God's own heart.

> David built houses for himself in the city of David. And he prepared a place for the ark of God and pitched a tent for it. Then David said that no one but the Levites may carry the ark of God, for the LORD had chosen them to carry the ark of the LORD and to minister to him forever. (1 Chron 15.1–2)

King David understood that God's silence was prohibitive. When the LORD specifically authorized the Levites to carry the ark of the covenant, all others were logically excluded. "No one but the Levites" was authorized, and God's silence was to be respected.

Further instructions had been authoritatively given by God concerning the transporting of the ark.

> You shall cast four rings of gold for it and put them on its four feet, two rings on the one side of it, and two rings on the other side of it. You shall make poles of acacia wood and overlay them with gold. And you shall put the poles into the rings on the sides of the ark to carry the ark by them. (Exod 25.12–14)

Though he was a man after God's own heart, when King David failed to respectfully follow the LORD's clear commandments concerning the carrying of the ark, disaster soon followed.

> David again gathered all the chosen men of Israel, thirty thousand. And David arose and went with all the people who were with him from Baale-judah to bring up from there the ark of God, which is called by the name of the LORD of hosts who sits enthroned on the cherubim. And they carried the ark of God on a new cart and brought it out of the house of Abinadab,

which was on the hill. And Uzzah and Ahio, the sons of Abi-nadab, were driving the new cart, with the ark of God, and Ahio went before the ark.

And David and all the house of Israel were making merry before the Lord, with songs and lyres and harps and tambou-rines and castanets and cymbals. And when they came to the threshing floor of Nacon, Uzzah put out his hand to the ark of God and took hold of it, for the oxen stumbled. And the anger of the Lord was kindled against Uzzah, and God struck him down there because of his error, and he died there beside the ark of God. And David was angry because the Lord had burst forth against Uzzah. And that place is called Perez-uzzah, to this day. And David was afraid of the Lord that day, and he said, "How can the ark of the Lord come to me?" So David was not willing to take the ark of the Lord into the city of David. But David took it aside to the house of Obed-edom the Gittite. And the ark of the Lord remained in the house of Obed-edom the Gittite three months, and the Lord blessed Obed-edom and all his household. (2 Sam 6.1–11)

God had never delivered a "thou shalt not" in respect to trans-porting the ark by cart. His law was silent in regard to methods other than poles on the sides of the ark. Was a deviation with good intentions accompanied by joyful praise a big deal? Listen to David's adapted perspective as he later spoke to the priests and heads of the fathers' houses of the Levites:

You are the heads of the Levitical families; you and your fellow Levites are to consecrate yourselves and bring up the ark of the Lord, the God of Israel, to the place I have prepared for it. It was because you, the Levites, did not bring it up the first time that the Lord our God broke out in anger against us. We did not inquire of him about how to do it in the prescribed way. (1 Chron 15.12–13, NIV).

There was a prescribed way to move the ark. When human beings didn't inquire of the Lord, but presumed for themselves, the consequences were dire. And they had no one to blame but themselves.

Years later, when the fame of King Uzziah—who was of the tribe of Judah—spread far, he overstepped the bounds of the law of God and was swiftly punished.

> But when he was strong, he grew proud, to his destruction. For he was unfaithful to the LORD his God and entered the temple of the LORD to burn incense on the altar of incense. But Azariah the priest went in after him, with eighty priests of the LORD who were men of valor, and they withstood King Uzziah and said to him, "It is not for you, Uzziah, to burn incense to the LORD, but for the priests, the sons of Aaron, who are consecrated to burn incense. Go out of the sanctuary, for you have done wrong, and it will bring you no honor from the LORD God." Then Uzziah was angry. Now he had a censer in his hand to burn incense, and when he became angry with the priests, leprosy broke out on his forehead in the presence of the priests in the house of the LORD, by the altar of incense. And Azariah the chief priest and all the priests looked at him, and behold, he was leprous in his forehead! And they rushed him out quickly, and he himself hurried to go out, because the LORD had struck him. And King Uzziah was a leper to the day of his death, and being a leper lived in a separate house, for he was excluded from the house of the LORD. (2 Chron 26.16–21)

The point of these, and so many other Old Testament accounts that could be listed, is plain. Thousands of years later, they scream out to us to be careful, to pay attention to what God has said, and to respect his silence.

> For the sons of Judah have done evil in my sight, declares the LORD. They have set their detestable things in the house that is called by my name, to defile it. And they have built the high places of Topheth, which is in the Valley of the Son of Hinnom, to burn their sons and their daughters in the fire, which I did not command, nor did it come into my mind. (Jer 7.30–31)

If God revealed it, it belonged to the people. Their responsibility was to act in accordance. If God didn't reveal it, the secret things were to be left to his prerogative. His silence was not to be regarded as a license for action.

> Everything that I command you, you shall be careful to do. You shall not add to it or take from it. (Deut 12.32)

New Testament Echoes of the Same Principles Behind God's Silence

We are not, on this historical side of the cross, under the authoritative scope of the Old Testament. At this point in God's eternal plan of redemption, we are not subject to the jurisdiction of the old law delivered through Moses. And yet, we shouldn't be surprised that the principles behind healthy respect for the Giver of all instruction and the Definer of all expectations would continue to resonate as foundational to "the law of liberty" (Jas 2.12). Fearful reverence for the silence of God is repeatedly prescribed for those who are "of Christ."

> Each of you should use whatever gift you have received to serve others, as faithful stewards of God's grace in its various forms. If anyone speaks, they should do so as one who speaks the very words of God. If anyone serves, they should do so with the strength God provides, so that in all things God may be praised through Jesus Christ. To him be the glory and the power for ever and ever. Amen. (1 Pet 4.10–11, NIV)

Could there be any humbler, safer, more reverent approach as created beings than to strive to speak where the Bible speaks and to remain silent where the Bible is silent? The apostle Paul made his strong appeals to the Christians in Corinth based on that foundational principle.

> I have applied all these things to myself and Apollos for your benefit, brothers, that you may learn by us not to go beyond what is written, that none of you may be puffed up in favor of one against another. For who sees anything different in you? What do you have that you did not receive? If then you received it, why do you boast as if you did not receive it? (1 Cor 4.6–7)

They were the recipients of God-breathed truth via Spirit-guided apostles. This truth didn't originate with any one saint or group of saints in Corinth. Men have boasted (and continue to boast) as if they are the originators of truth when, in fact, human beings are the recipients of truth as defined by the Creator. What then is our responsibility? To speak where God has spoken and remain silent where God is silent! Or, in the language of 1 Corinthians 4.1, "This is how one should regard us, as servants of Christ and stewards of the mysteries of God."

In the strongest of ways, John powerfully warns against ignoring the revealed will of God.

> I rejoiced greatly to find some of your children walking in the truth, just as we were commanded by the Father. And now I ask you, dear lady—not as though I were writing you a new commandment, but the one we have had from the beginning—that we love one another. And this is love, that we walk according to his commandments; this is the commandment, just as you have heard from the beginning, so that you should walk in it. For many deceivers have gone out into the world, those who do not confess the coming of Jesus Christ in the flesh. Such a one is the deceiver and the antichrist. Watch yourselves, so that you may not lose what we have worked for, but may win a full reward. Everyone who goes on ahead and does not abide in the teaching of Christ, does not have God. Whoever abides in the teaching has both the Father and the Son. If anyone comes to you and does not bring this teaching, do not receive him into your house or give him any greeting, for whoever greets him takes part in his wicked works. (2 John 4–11)

There is an objective body of truth described by a Spirit-led apostle as "the teaching of Christ." To step beyond it—either into that which is specifically forbidden, or into the unauthorized realm of silence—is to transgress the will of Almighty God. And whoever does so progresses without God.

When men of the first-century stepped beyond the teachings of the authoritative apostles, the transgression was recognized and rebuked. In Acts 15, in response to certain men from

Judea who were teaching Gentiles, "Unless you are circumcised according to the custom of Moses, you cannot be saved," the apostles and elders—with the whole church in Jerusalem—sent representatives to Antioch with a letter.

> The brothers, both the apostles and the elders, to the brothers who are of the Gentiles in Antioch and Syria and Cilicia, greetings. Since we have heard that some persons have gone out from us and troubled you with words, unsettling your minds, **although we gave them no instructions**, it has seemed good to us, having come to one accord, to choose men and send them to you with our beloved Barnabas and Paul, men who have risked their lives for the sake of our Lord Jesus Christ. (Acts 15.23–26)

The writer of Hebrews provides several illustrations which show how we ought to interact with the silence of God.

> Long ago, at many times and in many ways, God spoke to our fathers by the prophets, but in these last days he has spoken to us by his Son, whom he appointed the heir of all things, through whom also he created the world. He is the radiance of the glory of God and the exact imprint of his nature, and he upholds the universe by the word of his power. After making purification for sins, he sat down at the right hand of the Majesty on high, having become as much superior to angels as the name he has inherited is more excellent than theirs.
>   For to which of the angels did God ever say,
>
> "You are my Son,
>   today I have begotten you"?
>
> Or again,
>
> "I will be to him a father,
>   and he shall be to me a son"? (Heb 1.1–5)

In these last days, by God's design, we are to listen to his Son. Why? One of the inspired arguments is rooted in the silence of God.

In Hebrews 8.4, the writer affirms that Jesus could not function as a priest during his time on the earth. Why? He was of the tribe of Judah, not Levi.

> Now if perfection had been attainable through the Levitical priesthood (for under it the people received the law), what further need would there have been for another priest to arise after the order of Melchizedek, rather than one named after the order of Aaron? For when there is a change in the priesthood, there is necessarily a change in the law as well. For the one of whom these things are spoken belonged to another tribe, from which no one has ever served at the altar. For it is evident that our Lord was descended from Judah, and in connection with that tribe Moses said nothing about priests. (Heb 7.11–14)

In the Old Testament, it was an understood fact that no tribe other than Levi could install a priest to serve at the altar. In 1 Kings 12.31, Jeroboam "made temples on high places and appointed priests from among all the people, who were not of the Levites." Notice how his unlawful actions were soundly condemned in 1 Kings 13.1–2.

> And behold, a man of God came out of Judah by the word of the LORD to Bethel. Jeroboam was standing by the altar to make offerings. And the man cried against the altar by the word of the LORD and said, "O altar, altar, thus says the LORD: 'Behold, a son shall be born to the house of David, Josiah by name, and he shall sacrifice on you the priests of the high places who make offerings on you, and human bones shall be burned on you.'"

Why were Jeroboam's innovations condemned? Not because Moses had delivered in the law, "Thou shalt not appoint priests from Asher, Benjamin, Dan, Ephraim, Gad, Issachar, Judah, Manasseh, Naphtali, Reuben, Simeon or Zebulun." Moses was silent on the issue of priests coming from tribes other than Levi. And yet, Jeroboam was denounced and condemned because everyone knew the law said priests were to be from Levi (Num 3, 18).

In the New Testament, the writer of Hebrews reestablishes the fact that God had said nothing regarding priests from another tribe. Therefore, priests from any other tribe were naturally and logically forbidden. But in these last days, there is a change in the priesthood and, by necessity, a change in the law as well. It is evident that Jesus, our high priest, was of the tribe of Judah. The thunderous silence of God means something and the point could not be plainer!

Conclusion

When God wants his will carried out in a certain way, he is very specific in his instructions, whether he is referring to individual disciples or the organization, mission, work and methods of his church. If we truly love him with all of our hearts, then we will respect the silence of his revelation to mankind and limit ourselves to the guidance he has provided.

To speak where the Bible speaks and strive for silence where the Bible is silent is a noble goal worthy of our highest efforts and most steadfast dedication. When God's people wait for God's instructions so that they might fulfill God's purposes, God gets the glory.

Questions for Growth and Discussion

1. Have you heard people reason from the "Why can't we?" point-of-view when it comes to matters of service to God? If so, what were the issues? And why is "Why can't we?" an unstable foundation upon which to build our relationship with God?

2. How does the example of the men who were unclean at the time of the Passover in Numbers 9 demonstrate for us that the end does not justify the means?

3. Is Moses' response to their question in Numbers 9.8 still a valid approach for those who want to faithfully serve God? If not, why not? If so, why?

4. In Deuteronomy 29.29, when Moses said that "the secret things belong to the LORD our God," what did he mean? Is his statement still true and applicable to us today?

5. In 1 Chronicles 15.12–13, David explains that the anger of God had broken out against the people because they had not inquired of him about how to move the ark "in the prescribed way." What does he mean by "the prescribed way," and does God have a "prescribed way" for Christian life and service?

6. Why was King Uzziah afflicted by God with leprosy in 2 Chronicles 26.16–21?

7. How will our approach to everything be shaped if we resolve to speak "as one who speaks the very words of God" (1 Pet 4.10–11)?

8. In your own words, summarize John's point in 2 John 4–11.

9. Why was it a "big deal" that certain Jews were preaching the need for Gentiles to be circumcised, even though the apostles had given them no such instructions (Acts 15.24)?

10. Summarize how the writer of Hebrews reasons from a healthy respect for the silence of God.

twelve

How Should We Handle Tradition?

Perhaps you've heard the story of the young lady who, having recently returned from her honeymoon, was anxious to prepare a wonderful feast for her new husband in her new kitchen with her new pots and pans. Her husband noticed that as his lovely bride was preparing the ham she cut off a sizable portion of perfectly good meat and tossed it in the trash. Disturbed by his new wife's apparent wastefulness, the young husband quizzed the young lady as to why she would do such a thing. "I don't know," she replied, "that's what my mom always does."

Not willing to let the thing go, the young husband pushed and prodded until the new bride finally (in somewhat of a huff) decided to call her mother. "Surely mom will understand. I've seen her do it this way for years. It's got to be the *right* way to prepare a ham."

After hearing of her son-in-law's question, the mother laughed and told her daughter, "Your father asks me the same question every time he sees me fixing a ham. That's the way my mother always did it. I don't know why. It just is. And I've always thought I would ask her about it, but I keep forgetting. Why don't we call her now?"

The young newlywed and her mother arranged a three-way call to the matriarchal cook of the family who always seemed to have an answer for any question that would arise concerning the kitchen. The young bride, more than exasperated at this point and running increasingly behind schedule, quickly explained the silly concerns of her new husband. For the first time, the new-lywed's mother revealed to her own mother that she had been fielding and deflecting similar prying questions for years.

And the grandmother laughed. And laughed. And laughed.

"I had no idea, girls! Why, you've been throwing away perfectly good ham for decades! The only reason I ever cut the end of a ham off like that was because my pots and pans were never big enough to accommodate the hams I'd find at the grocery store!"

What had started off as an expedient way of preparing ham with smaller-than-ideal pots and pans had evolved over the span of two generations to, "This is the right way to prepare a ham," resulting in ignorant wastefulness. Granted, the daughter and granddaughter weren't looking to be wasteful or intending to be ignorant. They were simply mimicking what had been handed down to them, whether it made much personal, practical or economic sense at all.

An Age-Old Struggle for Balance and Harmony

In Matthew 15 we read of a confrontation involving the delicate balance between tradition and commandment.

> Then Pharisees and scribes came to Jesus from Jerusalem and said, "Why do your disciples break the tradition of the elders? For they do not wash their hands when they eat." He answered them, "And why do you break the commandment of God for the sake of your tradition?" (Matt 15.1–3)

Based on what we've seen throughout this study, the last thing any of us should ever want to hear is God's own Son diagnose us as breaking God's commandments, regardless of reason or motivation. If there is a God, and he does have a will for our lives, and he has communicated that will in understandable terms, and we will be held accountable to him based on what has been revealed, then we dare not ignore or break or dilute his commandments.

And yet, that is exactly what certain Pharisees and scribes of Jesus' day were guilty of doing. Why? For the sake of their tradition.

The dangerous premise has been established. The serious warning has been delivered. Human traditions can come to occupy such a place in the human heart that, for the sake of upholding and defending those traditions, a man or a woman will go so far as to break the commandments of God.

How, therefore, can we humbly and faithfully and consistently discern between the commandments of God and our own human traditions?

Key Terms Defined

"**Commandment,**" in the context of Matthew 15, refers to that which has been delivered to mankind via divine revelation. This becomes clear as we continue to read Matthew's account of the confrontation.

> For **God** commanded, "Honor your father and your mother," and, "Whoever reviles father or mother must surely die." But **you** say, "If anyone tells his father or his mother, 'What you would have gained from me is given to God,' he need not honor his father." So for the sake of **your** tradition **you** have made void **the word of God**. (Matt 15.4–6)

Jesus clearly delineated between the traditions of men and the "word of God." One had been delivered to mankind via divine revelation, and one had not.

Luke uses similar language in Luke 23.56 as he describes some of the female disciples at the tomb of Jesus.

> Then they returned and prepared spices and ointments. On the Sabbath they rested **according to the commandment**.

When terms like "commandment," "law," or "the word of God" are used in Scripture, they most often inherently represent an obligation God himself has imposed, under which human beings are amenable or accountable. If I, or you, or anyone else violates those divine edicts, we are guilty of sin.

> Everyone who makes a practice of sinning also practices lawlessness; sin is lawlessness. (1 John 3.4)

On the other hand, our English word **"tradition"** has old linguistic roots that literally refer to "instruction that has been handed down." It's a term that can certainly be used in very positive senses, framed by divine spokesmen in terms of God-sourced, authoritative instruction.

> Now I praise you because you remember me in everything and hold firmly to the **traditions**, just as I delivered them to you. (1 Cor 11.2, NASB)

> So then, brethren, stand firm and hold to the **traditions** which you were taught, whether by word of mouth or by letter from us. (2 Thes 2.15, NASB)

> Now we command you, brethren, in the name of our Lord Jesus Christ, that you keep away from every brother who leads an unruly life and not according to the **tradition** which you received from us. (2 Thes 3.6, NASB)

In this context, Paul was the divinely-chosen recipient of authoritative instruction from God. What was Paul's task? To take the information he had been provided and faithfully "hand it down" to others. In this sense, the information was divine tradition, and Paul described it as such in passages like 1 Corinthians 11.23—"For I received from the Lord what I also delivered to you." Paul had received important information from the Lord and was tasked with "handing it down" to saints in Corinth.

In his second letter to young Timothy, Paul used much the same line of reasoning.

> You then, my child, be strengthened by the grace that is in Christ Jesus, and what you have heard from me in the presence of many witnesses entrust to faithful men who will be able to teach others also. (2 Tim 2.1–2)

Paul had received important information from the Lord. He had carefully and faithfully communicated that information to Timothy. What, in turn, was Timothy's task? To carefully and faithfully entrust the information to even more men who would be able to keep the chain of vital information with a divine source alive and available.

In other situations, "tradition" is used in a very negative context to denote **human instruction** backed by **human authority** that clashes with and overshadows the rightful place of divine instruction backed by divine authority. Returning to our original text in Matthew 15:

> He answered them, "And why do you break the commandment of God for the sake of **your tradition**? For God commanded, 'Honor your father and your mother,' and, 'Whoever reviles father or mother must surely die.' But you say, 'If anyone tells his father or his mother, "What you would have gained from me is given to God," he need not honor his father.' So for the sake of your tradition you have made void the word of God. You hypocrites! Well did Isaiah prophesy of you, when he said:
>
> 'This people honors me with their lips,
>   but their heart is far from me;
> in vain do they worship me,
>   teaching as doctrines the **commandments of men**.'"
>
> (Matt 15.7–9)

The problem? Human instruction and authority usurped divine instruction and authority. Paul sounded the same warning.

> See to it that no one takes you captive by philosophy and empty deceit, according to **human tradition**, according to the elemental spirits of the world, and not according to Christ. (Col 2.8)

Obviously, the use and import of "tradition" as it appears in Scripture depends upon its context. From a negative standpoint, the fundamental danger in dealing with human traditions is personally treating them or binding them on others as if they were delivered by God himself. Such can become "burdens" that are unnecessarily levied on people, robbing them of legitimate freedom and expedient leeway available in Christ.

They (the scribes and Pharisees of Jesus' day) tie up heavy burdens, hard to bear, and lay them on people's shoulders, but they themselves are not willing to move them with their finger. (Matt 23.4)

Of primary importance is an honest evaluation of our mission and methods and motivation using some straightforward questions:

From what source is this information or practice or custom drawing its authority?

As we humbly and objectively trace the pathway of this information or practice or custom backward from generation to generation, what bedrock do we eventually hit? Whose idea was it to try this thing in this way? A man's or God's?

Is this information or practice or custom of divine origin? Or, in the name of expediency, did it come to exist as one of many human methods that can be employed to meet a divine ideal?

Why are we trying to accomplish _____ via this approach?

I may believe _____ should be done in this way. But why? Why am I concerned with encouraging others to do the same thing in the same way?

I may even believe that _____ is the *only* way to accomplish _____. But can I point to divine authority as the basis of binding this approach?

The Need for Spiritual Discernment

In an effort to faithfully judge between the words of God and human traditions, certain fundamental principles must be consistently remembered and employed.

1. The will of God was made known through people who were credentialed by miraculous signs. Moses gave the old Jewish law (John 1.17). Supernatural phenomena confirmed the authoritative validity behind Moses' transmission of the will of God.

On the morning of the third day there were thunders and lightnings and a thick cloud on the mountain and a very loud trumpet blast, so that all the people in the camp trembled. Then Moses brought the people out of the camp to meet God, and they took their stand at the foot of the mountain. Now Mount Sinai was wrapped in smoke because the LORD had descended on it in fire. The smoke of it went up like the smoke of a kiln, and the whole mountain trembled greatly. And as the sound of the trumpet grew louder and louder, Moses spoke, and God answered him in thunder. The LORD came down on Mount Sinai, to the top of the mountain. And the LORD called Moses to the top of the mountain, and Moses went up. (Exod 19.16–20)

Now the appearance of the glory of the LORD was like a devouring fire on the top of the mountain in the sight of the people of Israel. Moses entered the cloud and went up on the mountain. And Moses was on the mountain forty days and forty nights. (Exod 24.17–18)

When Moses came down from Mount Sinai, with the two tablets of the testimony in his hand as he came down from the mountain, Moses did not know that the skin of his face shone because he had been talking with God. Aaron and all the people of Israel saw Moses, and behold, the skin of his face shone, and they were afraid to come near him. But Moses called to them, and Aaron and all the leaders of the congregation returned to him, and Moses talked with them. Afterward all the people of Israel came near, and he commanded them all that the LORD had spoken with him in Mount Sinai. (Exod 34.29–32)

Such supernatural phenomena forced the children of Israel to a point of decision—would they believe Moses' words and follow his lead, however challenging the journey, or would they ignore the signs and refuse to follow? The signs that accompanied the authoritative message removed any excuse for disobedience.

"The law was given through Moses; grace and truth came through Jesus Christ. No one has ever seen God; the only God, who is at the Father's side, he has made him known" (John 1.17–

18). The new law—the law of liberty (Jas 1.25; 2.12)—came through Jesus Christ and was also validated by miracles.

> Now Jesus did many other signs in the presence of the disciples, which are not written in this book; but these are written so that you may believe that Jesus is the Christ, the Son of God, and that by believing you may have life in his name. (John 20.30–31)

The miracles of Jesus forced people to a point of decision— would they believe his words, however challenging the demands, or would they ignore the signs and refuse the message? A classic case study is John 11, when Jesus raised Lazarus from the dead.

> Many of the Jews therefore, who had come with Mary and had seen what he did, believed in him, but some of them went to the Pharisees and told them what Jesus had done. So the chief priests and the Pharisees gathered the Council and said, "What are we to do? For this man performs many signs. If we let him go on like this, everyone will believe in him, and the Romans will come and take away both our place and our nation." But one of them, Caiaphas, who was high priest that year, said to them, "You know nothing at all. Nor do you understand that it is better for you that one man should die for the people, not that the whole nation should perish." He did not say this of his own accord, but being high priest that year he prophesied that Jesus would die for the nation, and not for the nation only, but also to gather into one the children of God who are scattered abroad. So from that day on they made plans to put him to death. (John 11.45–53)

Clearly, the authoritative validity behind Jesus' claim to be the Messiah was confirmed by supernatural phenomena, and such phenomena forced the descendants of Abraham to a point of decision—would they believe his words and follow his lead, however challenging the demands, or would they ignore the signs and seek to eliminate him by whatever means necessary? The signs that accompanied the authoritative message removed any excuse for disobedience and, consequently, revealed the darkened state of the self-centered hearts of the chief priests and Pharisees.

Likewise, the miracles subsequently performed by the Spirit-empowered appointees of Jesus validated the divine origin of the New Testament. In Acts 3.6, Peter said to a certain man lame from birth, "In the name of Jesus Christ of Nazareth, rise up and walk!" Immediately the feet and ankles of the lame man were made strong.

> While he clung to Peter and John, all the people, utterly astounded, ran together to them in the portico called Solomon's. And when Peter saw it he addressed the people: "Men of Israel, why do you wonder at this, or why do you stare at us, as though by our own power or piety we have made him walk? The God of Abraham, the God of Isaac, and the God of Jacob, the God of our fathers, glorified his servant Jesus, whom you delivered over and denied in the presence of Pilate, when he had decided to release him. But you denied the Holy and Righteous One, and asked for a murderer to be granted to you, and you killed the Author of life, whom God raised from the dead. To this we are witnesses. And his name—by faith in his name—has made this man strong whom you see and know, and the faith that is through Jesus has given the man this perfect health in the presence of you all." (Acts 3.11–16).

It was not a coincidence at this point that Peter moved the attention of the people from the miracle to the message of the gospel.

> "And now, brothers, I know that you acted in ignorance, as did also your rulers. But what God foretold by the mouth of all the prophets, that his Christ would suffer, he thus fulfilled. Repent therefore, and turn again, that your sins may be blotted out, that times of refreshing may come from the presence of the Lord, and that he may send the Christ appointed for you, Jesus, whom heaven must receive until the time for restoring all the things about which God spoke by the mouth of his holy prophets long ago." (Acts 3.17–21)

An indisputable miracle confirmed the authoritative validity behind Peter's call to repentance, and the miracle forced the inhabitants of Jerusalem to a point of decision—would they believe his words and respond in repentance, however challenging that repentance may be, or would they ignore the miracle and continue to live in whatever way they chose, believing whatever they chose to believe? The sign that accompanied the authoritative call to repentance removed any excuse for disobedience.

"Many of those who had heard the word believed, and the number of the men came to about five thousand" (Acts 4.4). But Acts 4.16–18 once again gives us a window into the darkened hearts of the self-centered rulers and elders and scribes of Jerusalem.

> What shall we do with these men? For that a notable sign has been performed through them is evident to all the inhabitants of Jerusalem, and we cannot deny it. But in order that it may spread no further among the people, let us warn them not to speak or teach at all in the name of Jesus.

Clearly, the authoritative validity behind the claims of Jesus and his apostles continued to be confirmed by supernatural phenomena, and such phenomena would continue to force these rulers to a point of decision. What was their decision?

> They called [Peter and John] and charged them not to speak or to teach at all in the name of Jesus. But Peter and John answered them, "Whether it is right in the sight of God to listen to you rather than to God, you must judge, for we cannot but speak of what we have seen and heard." And when they had further threatened them, they let them go, finding no way to punish them, because of the people, for all were praising God for what had happened. For the man on whom this sign of healing was performed was more than forty years old. (Acts 4.18–22)

The miracles confirmed the authoritative validity of the message and forced people to the point of decision. In both the Old and New Testaments, the will of God was made known through people who were credentialed by miraculous signs. The Bible is more—so much more—than the outdated ideas and irrelevant opinions and obsolete cultural preferences of old Christians. These men "spoke from God as they were carried along by the Holy Spirit" (2 Pet 1.21).

But mere human traditions—whether they be national, communal, congregational, familial, or personal—do not carry such weight. They have been handed down, perhaps for many generations, but their ultimate source is not divine. They are useful and helpful and sometimes sentimental, but they are not—as defined by God—exclusive or binding on all people of all nationalities and cultures and times. Human traditions are not handed down by people credentialed by miraculous signs.

How very foolish, therefore, to treat human instructions backed by nothing but human authority as though they were the words of God himself! How arrogant to bind human traditions on others as if they carried the weight of divine authority! There is nothing inherently wrong with tradition. Every generation "hands down" certain personal preferences, expedient methods and useful tools to accomplish future tasks. But the will of God was made known through people who were credentialed by miraculous signs. Human tradition carries no such weight.

2. Sacred communication is not amenable, conformable, or compliant to human alteration. This bring us full circle, back to the initial premises of this study. When it comes to God's communication, my responsibility is not to tweak it or make it relevant or more palatable for my own generation and cultural. If God is the source, my responsibility is to learn, to obey and to share what I've discovered with others.

> You shall not add to the word that I command you, nor take from it, that you may keep the commandments of the LORD your God that I command you. (Deut 4.2)

> Every word of God proves true;
>   he is a shield to those who take refuge in him.
> Do not add to his words,
>   lest he rebuke you and you be found a liar.
>   (Prov 30.5–6)

I warn everyone who hears the words of the prophecy of this book: if anyone adds to them, God will add to him the plagues described in this book, and if anyone takes away from the words of the book of this prophecy, God will take away his share in the tree of life and in the holy city, which are described in this book. (Rev 22.18–19)

Sacred communication remains applicable to all who are under its jurisdiction, as long as the source of authority designed it to last.

"Do not think that I have come to abolish the Law or the Prophets; I have not come to abolish them but to fulfill them. For truly, I say to you, until heaven and earth pass away, not an iota, not a dot, will pass from the Law until all is accomplished." (Matt 5.17–18)

And Jesus came and said to them, "All authority in heaven and on earth has been given to me. Go therefore and make disciples of all nations, baptizing them in the name of the Father and of the Son and of the Holy Spirit, teaching them to observe all that I have commanded you. And behold, I am with you always, to the end of the age." (Matt 28.18–20)

Human tradition isn't like that. Human tradition evolves. Human tradition is established by human habits and human customs. It will vary in its character from place to place and time to time. What may have been judged and employed as expedient fifty years ago very well may, upon honest and humble evaluation, be set aside for something even more expedient or helpful in the present situation. A practice or custom that has been entrenched and even taken for granted over the course of several decades in one culture may not be adopted and employed by the inhabitants of another culture in another time. And that's alright because human tradition is established by human habits and human customs with human authority.

Once again, human tradition is not intrinsically evil. It operates in the realm of expediency and human judgment. But it is to be rebuked and reprioritized when it is thrust into the role of and bound on others as divine law.

Conclusion

May God be patient with us and help us to recognize the two very real "ditches" into which we so frequently fall when traveling the highway of discernment and obedience.

1. The tendency to carelessly reduce sacred communication to the status of human tradition.

2. The disposition that would arrogantly turn and bind human tradition into something resembling sacred communication.

Both ditches along the highway are wrong, and those who have lost their way in either direction must be lovingly, yet firmly, directed toward a more accurate handling of God's revealed will. At the end of the day (and the end of time) few things can be accurately classified as more serious than breaking the commandments of God for the sake of our traditions and teaching as doctrines the commandments of men.

Questions for Growth and Discussion

1. List some ways that human beings have been guilty of reducing sacred communication to the status of human tradition.

2. List some ways that human beings have been guilty of turning and binding human tradition into something resembling sacred communication.

---*thirteen*---

Conclusion

Isaiah 66.1–2 contains an awesome promise.

Thus says the LORD:

"Heaven is my throne,
  and the earth is my footstool;
what is the house that you would build for me,
  and what is the place of my rest?
All these things my hand has made,
  and so all these things came to be,
    declares the LORD.
But this is the one to whom I will look:
  he who is humble and contrite in spirit
  and trembles at my word."

On what more appropriate note could we end than that? In our culture of extreme subjectivity and doubt, let us be men and women of God who are confident in relation to divine truth, standing strong in the strength which the Lord supplies. In the words of Francis Schaeffer, "The ordinary Christian with the Bible in his hand can say that the majority is wrong." With Christlike motives in our hearts and God's word as our guide, may we never be afraid to do so.

And as a compliment to godly confidence, may we never forget our Lord's call to humility. In lowly dependence of spirit, may we never fail to tremble at the word of God. Homer Hailey is reported to have said on more than one occasion, "The Bible is like a mighty ocean whose vast depths no one can ever fully explore, but in whose shallow waters even the smallest child may safely wade."

My aim is to swim as deeply and joyfully as possible in that vast ocean for the rest of my life, always seeking to maintain childlike wonder at the breadth and depth of God's wisdom and majesty. I hope your heart is moved to do the same.

Also By Jason Hardin

Boot Camp
Equipping Men with Integrity for Spiritual Warfare

Boot Camp is where a soldier is equipped for the battles ahead and where he learns from the veterans of previous wars. Boot Camp: Equipping Men with Integrity for Spiritual Warfare is the first volume in the new IMAGE series of books for men by Jason Hardin. It serves as a Basic Training manual in the spiritual war for honor, integrity and a God-glorifying life. 237 pages, $13.99 (PB); $24.99 (HB).

"This is a great book to help us men live opposite of this world's model of a man."

Stephen Arterburn
Best-Selling Author, including *Every Man's Battle*

Hard Core
Defeating Sexual Temptation with a Superior Satisfaction

So many—men and women included—are being slaughtered in their struggle with sexual sin. Individual lives, marriages, children, influences for good, ministries of gospel preachers, and entire congregations of the Lord's people are being seriously impacted. If we are going to win this battle, we must strike at the root of the problem. We must sound the call for righteous warfare. We must dedicate ourselves to hardcore holiness and fight sexual temptation with a superior satisfaction. 106 pages, $7.99 (PB).

Defeating Sexual Temptation with a Superior Satisfaction
Jason Hardin

Churches of the New Testament
Ethan Longhenry

Have you ever wondered what it would be like to be a Christian in the first century? What would it be like to meet with the church in Philippi or Ephesus? What would go on in their assemblies? Churches of the New Testament explores the world of first century Christianity by examining what Scripture reveals about the local churches of God's people. It examines background information about the geography and history of each city, as well as whatever is known about the founding of the church there. This book also considers what happened to the church after the first century. Centuries may separate us from the churches of the New Testament, but their examples, instruction, commendation, and rebukes can teach us today. 150 pages. $9.99 (PB)

Flight Paths: A Devotional Guide for Your Journey
Dene Ward

When encroaching blindness took her music teaching career away, Dene Ward turned her attention to writing. What began as e-mail devotions to some friends grew into a list of hundreds of subscribers. Three hundred sixty-six of those devotions have been assembled to form this daily devotional. Follow her through a year of camping, bird-watching, medical procedures, piano lessons, memories, and more as she uses daily life as a springboard to thought-provoking and character-challenging messages of endurance and faith. 475 pages. $18.99 (PB).

Things Most Surely Believed
Forrest D. Moyer

In these 16 brief sermons, Forrest Darrell Moyer has stated with beautiful clarity and simplicity, yet with compelling force, the Christian's "reason for hope" that is in him. He deals with the greatest themes the race has ever known—God, Christ, the cross, sin and redemption, the church, heaven and hell—yet he does it in language that the man in the pew, unskilled in the intricacies of theological vocabularies, can easily grasp. These sermons partake of that same quality which characterized the initial preaching of the gospel by Christ himself, of whom it was said, "and the common people heard him gladly." Foreword by Doy Moyer. New Introduction by Jefferson David Tant. 142 pages. $9.99 (PB)

HERITAGE
OF FAITH LIBRARY

The **DeWard Publishing Company Heritage of Faith Library** is a growing collection of classic Christian reprints. DeWard has already published or has plans to publish the following authors:

- A. B. Bruce
- Atticus G. Haygood
- H. C. Leupold
- J. W. McGarvey
- William Paley
- Albertus Pieters

Future authors and titles added to this series will be announced on our website, where you will also find a full listing of DeWard Publishing titles:

www.deward.com

DEWARD
PUBLISHING COMPANY

CPSIA information can be obtained
at www.ICGtesting.com
Printed in the USA
JSRBC011555161120
JK10491200001B/2